Promises of Shirdi Sai Baba
The Eleven Pre

Bela Sharma

STERLING PAPERBACKS
An imprint of
Sterling Publishers (P) Ltd.
Regd. Office: A1/256 Safdarjung Enclave,
New Delhi-110029. CIN: U22110DL1964PTC211907
Tel: 26387070, 26386209; Fax: 91-11-26383788
E-mail: mail@sterlingpublishers.com
www.sterlingpublishers.com

Promises of Shirdi Sai Baba: The Eleven Precious Sayings
© 2016, Bela Sharma
ISBN 978 93 85913 98 3

All rights are reserved.
No part of this publication may be reproduced, stored in a retrieval system or transmitted, in any form or by any means, mechanical, photocopying, recording or otherwise, without prior written permission of the original publisher.

Printed in India

Printed and Published by Sterling Publishers Pvt. Ltd.,
Plot No. 13, Ecotech-III, Greater Noida - 201306,
Uttar Pradesh, India

DEDICATION

All is offered at the Lotus Feet of Lord Sai Baba, my entire self is dedicated to Him, for Him. You alone, O Sai, are the sole doer, we are simply obeying your orders. The doer, deed, sequence of events in life, fruit of all actions—all are your forms and it is you alone who takes all to fruition by making, we mortals, mere means. So we offer all that is granted by You at Your Lotus Feet. We offer our body, mind, maya, our breath, life, death, all events of our life, the ways of the body and the soul, at Your Lotus Feet. By Your Grace alone we get a new direction to move towards your divine reality.

Promises of Shirdi Sai Baba
The Eleven Precious Sayings

The promises granted to us by Lord Sai are precious, as they guide the Human race towards a direction that is unique, amazing and towards the Lord alone.

It is the words of Lord Brahma, that write our destiny, The Lord's words alone pave the path of love and devotion.

Not for just one or two or for you and me but for all, for many.

In our entire lifetime we either fall on the threshold of sorrow, pain or pride or move with confidence on the grounds of happiness, politeness or it's a joyful ride.

The Lord's assurances, saturated with love, ferry us to unseen, Divine Horizons as though getting us face to face with our own real selves, granting us our true identity.

The Lord's words are deeper than the sea, Vaster than vastness (the sky).

They radiate the divine glitter of the sun, Filling us with satiation and quenching our thirst as droplets of divine rain.

They smile on us as flowers, bathing this vagrant mind with their annihilating fragrance.

Whenever the Lord incarnates on the earth, our progress is assured.

Binding Himself in the parameters of the body, the Lord shows us the true path.

By His words, deeds, leelas, He makes our inner-self blossom.

He is elated to awaken the sleeping faith and humanity inside us, by the soothing breeze of His love, touch and joy.

We mortals bathe in this joy after adorning the elating direction tapped inside us by the Lord.

We try to play on the dormant strings of devotion, love and faith by the ragas of the Lord's name

Life goes on, based fully on the 'Words of the Lord' which are saturated with faith, a state which, too, has been generated by Him alone.

We mortals fill our lives with the stability of these pillars of faith.

Holding these pillars with a sure self, filled with full dedication, love and faith, we bathe in His divine devotional love.

He makes us reach the unseen, untouched shores that are beyond our imagination.

The 'light of faith' flows to us as nectar through the 'precious promises' made by the Lord.

The simple straight words uttered by the Lord are a means to unfurl the depth inside each one of us (an integral part of all of us) and it is this nectar that brings to light, deep secrets hidden inside us.

We have to savour this nectar and we have to flow in and with the flow of this Grace.

We have to fill our inner self with this, Godly Divine Light by awakening the true self immersed in the darkness of Maya.

So that there is Divine awakening and our inner self illuminates.

Holding on firmly to the promises of the Lord, On the threshold of the pillars of firm unflinching faith, we realize our true self.

By adorning the Divine Light, We attain divinity and glitter in the pious Ganges of Sai Baba's precious promises.

In this amazing Mansion of life, filled with love and faith, which is standing firmly on the pillars of His Name,

We do attain our true self.

By crossing the Ocean of Mundane existence, we embrace deliverance.

We adorn Moksha!

So be it!
Om Sai Ram

Introduction

Sai Baba's 'precious sayings' are not mere words written in a book, but are 'promises' that *He* has made to His devotees, promises that He has always stood by and made us experience. Devotees experience the authenticity of these promises at every step of their lives. Each word uttered by Lord Sai is, in fact, Lord's own Vani or Brahma Vakya, which we have to assimilate to the depths of our heart and bathe in blissful joy, once we understand the same.

Baba's precious words are our treasure which we have been accumulating over many births. Each promise is drenched with love and filled with pure, pious feelings. These precious promises are for each living being, entire humanity, in fact, for the human race itself.

For example, we promise our children that if they do all tasks in life at the right time, in the right way, under our guidance and supervision, then we will surely reward them and their good deeds will bear fruit in the form of the Lord's Grace in their journey of life. In the same way, Lord Sai has given us different tasks to perform and our Lord Sai is so kind that even before we execute the tasks assigned to us with full honesty or before we complete them, Baba has already, that is, in advance, rewarded us in the form of His eleven promises or sayings. We have to peep within, search our inner self, to know if we have been able to gather, assimilate, adorn ourselves with His Grace, His divine love that is flowing ceaselessly from His promises. Are we ready to be rewarded by the kind Lord Almighty?

Before adorning and imbibing His Grace, in the form of His promises, and hence bathing in their joy, let us first dive deeply into these eleven pious sayings and make an attempt to understand Baba's deep, divine messages hidden in them. Let us try to get a feel of the deeper message, assimilate the same and make these messages an integral part of our lives. Only after this attempt will we be able to see and analyse if are we still crawling, walking, standing still on the path of love and devotion or are we actually running, understanding and imbibing, that is, running on the path paved by these eleven sacred paths, and hence soaking the shower of His love fully. Let us dive deep into these eleven sayings and find our own true identity, by His Grace.

Bela Sharma
A-3/154, Janakpuri,
New Delhi-110058
Mobile: 9868867940

Salutations

Lord Ganpati smiled on us as the one who removes all obstacles, Godess Saraswati showered pearls from Her pen. The blessings of all Gods and Demigods radiated Divine colour and the Lord's form smiled in words. Friends and relatives always helped in their own ways, Nature too showered 'Nectar' for human upliftment. My husband Vinod Sharma, son Animesh and daughter Anushree encouraged me at every step. They acted as the Lords' angels guiding my path towards my true mission of life—spreading the Lords name. My mother Swaran Nanda and father Dharmendra Pratap Nanda's blessings blossomed as words. Lord Dattatrey's Golden Love radiated all around as Brahma, Vishnu and Mahesha. Through the medium of His eleven sayings or promises, our Lord, our all, Sai Baba put a stamp of His Divine Grace on us. His unending, unparalleled love and affection, He showered on us with an open Heart and with full Divine joy. My salutations to one and all, probably are beyond words.

Contents

1. First Promise 13
2. Second Promise 21
3. Third Promise 29
4. Fourth Promise 37
5. Fifth Promise 45
6. Sixth Promise 53
7. Seventh Promise 61
8. Eighth Promise 69
9. Ninth Promise 77
10. Tenth Promise 85
11. Eleventh Promise 93

First Promise

One who steps on the soil of Shirdi,
All His difficulties will be warded off.

This means that one who steps on the pure soil of Shirdi, all his sufferings will come to an end.

Shirdi is that pious land on which Sai Baba, an incarnation of Lord Dattatreya—the Trinity God, appeared for the benefit, for the upliftment of His devotees. An incarnation that was and is fully for His devotees, bound to the love and devotion of His devotees. The land on which the Lord incarnates bound to a mortal coil, is called the Karma Kshetra, resting place, home or place for this particular form to operate from, to spread the name, love, message of God, far and wide.

As we stay comfortably with a sense of complete security in our homes, similarly we feel overtly secure in the home that the Lord has chosen for His incarnated form, the place which is known as His Karya Khshetra or a place from where He will perform the bodily deeds through the incarnated self.

On the path of life, in a web of Karmas, we may go to innumerable places, may perform many tasks through the day, go to big places for celebrations in life, wear expensive clothes, adorn ourselves with a layer of make up, put a smile on our face to keep smiling even if we don't feel like—this is life. But once we are back home, we get rid of all this artificial paraphernalia to be in the most comfortable clothes, without the outward artificiality—we are our true self, very comfortable. We may experience joy in this world but true comfort we only feel in our homes.

Same happens with our life. We keep performing deeds on this path of life, a life granted by the Lord, yet in this flow of Karmas we tend to forget the basis of life, the Lord, who is actually holding the reins of our life. We are lost in the scintillating effect produced by Maya and lost in the flow of our own Karmic cycle. So our moving out of our houses with all kind of material adornment actually depicts our artificial life. A life which has been fully covered by Maya and entanglement of Karmas, hence making it fully artificial.

During the course of this mortal journey when we go to Shirdi, we are actually entering the realms of our "true home". Shirdi is that pious land which was the home adorned by the incarnation of the Lord God Himself—Sai Baba, to bless us with His Leelas. We get a very different kind of comfort, a rare contentment fills our heart, when we go to Shirdi. Its only because of this different, amazing and pious feel that our pure, real self surfaces once we touch the soil of Shirdi. We are peaceful, an amazing peace fills us, a wondrous joy engulfs us and we experience that even today, in the horrendous pace of life there is a piece of land on this earth that is a part of the same, yet totally different, as it is amazingly, differently, pious and pure. It is this satiation, this peace, the feel of true contentment that gives us a feel of our own true selves, a feel that we experience the minute we touch this pious land— SHIRDI. This pious land gets us face to face with our true self, where the artificial faces of this mortal coil are shed off one by one, those innumerable artificial faces adorned by us due to the frightening pace of Maya. That is why Baba has said:

"One who steps on the soil of Shirdi, his sufferings will come to an end."

Shirdi is our "true home", our true destination, where we get a feel of our true self, free of all worries and devoid of artificiality, we can see and make an attempt to understand our true selves under the protective care of the Lord by piercing the artificial face of Maya, purely by His Grace. Here, under the shade of this pious Guru God Sai we are able to develop our "true identity". Once we have shed off our artificial self, i.e., the artificiality which is the true reality, speciality of Maya by playing on the strings of our true identity, awakening it with the waves of devotion and love. When we make an attempt to be one with our own true selves, when we try to shed off the bondages of this mortal coil and make an attempt to adorn the soul, then it is natural that our bodily difficulties will start declining as sorrow, pain, torture are characteristics of this body, they are entirely bodily effects. The Atman is beyond and much above all these and pain can't even touch the soul.

So the one who touches the pious land of Shirdi has actually stepped on the threshold of the soul, has got an entry into the fragrant basis of the soul, undoubtedly the sorrows of such a being come to an end. The mortal being who reaches Shirdi, is actually moving closer to the Shirdi within, Shedding off the bodily sorrow and pain to adorn the Lord Himself, by making our soul a means to reach the Lord, as the soul within signifies the Shirdi inside us. Make these bodily digressions a means to get rid of Maya or suffering, step on the pious soil of Shirdi try to recognize and understand your true self, seated inside you by shedding the bodily digressions in the Lord's Lotus feet on the pious land of Shirdi and be rapt in atmic elation or the divine flight of the soul. Try to understand the true value and need of this body, make it a means to recognise the soul within, to ultimately merge into the Lord Almighty, hence embracing deliverance.

To quote an example—when we cook something then whatever be its taste, smell or flavour, its true mission is to quench our hunger. Similarly the Lord is Omnipresent but when the Lotus feet of His incarnated self touch any pious piece of land, its only then that we mortals, bound by the bondages of this body, are able to see, understand and hence assimilate Him in that particular form, to be able to take a spiritual flight, a divine take off.

The Lord's Grace is felt the minute we touch the soil of Shirdi—some feel that their long stuck up work was accomplished and some are lost in the flow of divine vibrations they receive from here. A child may be far from his mother but he always gets her feel whenever he remembers her but when he is close to her, in her close proximity, then the flow of love and protection he gets in his mothers arms is far superior to just her thought. Similarly going to Shirdi is like getting the mothers embrace, though we were never deprived of her love even while we were far away.

So going to Shirdi is like adorning the loving, protective embrace of one's mother, this does not mean that we are deprived of Sai Maa's love, even if we are far from Shirdi. Going to Shirdi sheds off our artificial self to a great extent and we move closer to our own true self. All our pain and sorrow surface due to our own artificial, cunning self, so if we shed off this artificial self, that our pain and sorrow vanish, automatically. So all artificiality is shed off when we go to Shirdi, and we enter the realms of our own true self. We dance in the joy of our spiritual enhancement, hence shedding off difficulties, pain.

By this saying, is Baba trying to tell us that He only resides in Shirdi and our sufferings are put to an end only when we step on the pious soil of Shirdi? Is the Lord not Omnipresent? Does He not reach out to His devotees when they call out in despair, anytime from anywhere on this earth? On the other hand those who live on the pious soil of Shirdi—do they never suffer bodily? No, it is not possible. Those living in or away from Shirdi—all equally atone for their deeds. At the same time whether in Shirdi or away from Shirdi whenever Baba's loved ones cry out in despair, they are undoubtedly, instantaneously showered by His Grace and love, as God always—anywhere and everywhere does reward one's deeds, i.e., Karma and Bhakti—they automatically get their due, i.e., His Grace. Then why do our sufferings come to an end when we step on the pure soil of Shirdi? Is Shirdi merely a piece of land in Maharashtra, is it a magical paradise on earth—where, once we put our feet, all our sufferings come to an end? What is Shirdi?

Shirdi is the pure threshold of our true, pious unblemished inner self. Shirdi is the self illuminative Brahmand inside each one of us. When we talk of putting an end to our suffering by stepping on the pure soil of Shirdi, we are actually talking of turning our thoughts, our vision, our entire self inwards to the light inside us—this is the real meaning of stepping on the soil of Shirdi. Turn your vision inside your own self to achieve the true self within, even while dwelling in this mortal coil. Once you are in tune with your true, divine, inner self then even while dwelling in the body, the bodily digressions do not hinder the divinity from within to reflect all around, from the inside to the outside. Our body is constantly moving towards digression, while the soul, rapt in the Lord Almighty, attains "elation" to the unknown undiscovered horizons. So suffering is due to the bodily digression and Karmic recycling. But even amid this bodily digression if we are in tune with our inner self, i.e., with the Lord dwelling inside us, we turn our vision to the Shirdi within, then slowly, with the passage of time the pious Shirdi inside each one of us keeps putting a stamp to our growing faith in the same, hence making our faith firm and unshakable. So even while dwelling in the body and suffering bodily, we are always in a state of "Divine Bliss" as we are fully linked with the Shirdi within in such a way, that outwardly we are in tune with the world but internally, actually, we are always in Shirdi, i.e., in tune with our "true" inner self. So Shirdi is the divine in each one of us and once we are fully aware and always on the pure soil of this inner Divine Self then how can bodily suffering really deter us from this path or affect us in any way?

As the link between you and your inner self blooms, i.e., as the Shirdi inside you grows and strengthens, proportionately you will be liberated from the sufferings of the outside world. That is why Baba said, "one who steps on the pious soil of Shirdi, his sufferings will come to an end." To find an entry into the Shirdi within each one of us, our journey starts from the Shirdi in Maharashtra, as we are bodily beings, so we start from a place where we can go bodily, then slowly this outward Shirdi leads us to the Shirdi within, hence putting an end to the feel of the bodily suffering, we may be anywhere on this earth, Baba is "always" with us, but when we go to

Shirdi, i.e., the pious land in Maharashtra, Sai Baba showers His Divine Grace on us, in such abundance that we straight away find an uninterrupted entry into the Shirdi within.

Living anywhere in the world and praying to Sai is like making a detailed plan of our life, but once we step on the soil of Shirdi the plan gets a proper stamp—is endorsed by "Sai Naam" and once the green signal is given in the form of the stamp then there is no problem in executing the same, i.e., entering, enjoying and always living in the realms of the Shirdi inside us, where bodily sufferings are like passing clouds which only give us a cool feel, cool breeze and move on.

So before its too late, this body ditches you at the last moment, enter into the realms of the Shirdi within, hence getting rid of all bodily suffering, merge and be rapt with the joy within, losing your identity to the "Sai" seated in the Shirdi inside you. So the one who enters the Shirdi inside ones own self, such a one would undoubtedly attain "Sai" by shedding off outward bodily sufferings, attaining never ending happiness, peace, satiation, will merge or be one with the Omnipotent Lord Almighty. We will actually attain the true mission of our life—the Lord God of Shirdi, attaining the Lord in the Shirdi within, hence adorning deliverance and will be finally liberated.

So be it!
Om Sai Ram!

Second Promise

Climbing the steps of the Samadhi,
Generations of sorrow and suffering shall cease.

One who steps on any one of the three steps of the Samadhi is actually crushing generations of sorrow under his or her feet.

To climb up to the pious Samadhi and to reach inside the safe arms of the Dwarkamaayi one has to step on three steps, hence to reach the desired resting place. These three steps, in both the uplifting destinations, i.e., Samadhi Mandir and Dwarkamaayi depict the three stages of life—childhood, youth and old age. To cross the border, the threshold of life, to be enhanced from the body to the soul, to enter into the realms of spirituality, Bliss and liberation or moksha one has to cross the three stages traversed by this body, by making these three stages a means for our final deliverance, for the attainment of God. It is not possible to realize the Lord Almighty, to attain self-realization or liberation till one has not traversed all the stages of life with full dedication and honesty.

Life is a continuous process, not only a means to square up our old-debts but a platform to build up good, positive deeds so that with every step in life, we keep shedding off the bondages of the body, hence enhancing to higher spiritual realms, i.e., the upliftment of the soul towards the super soul. At every juncture in life, while atoning for our deeds, if we keep shedding off bad thoughts or negativity and keep moving on the path of atmic elation with the power of His Name and His Divine Grace, then surely we are putting an end to our sorrows and are building a positive spiritual journey, even while dwelling in this body. The three steps leading to the Samadhi are actually the three divisions or stages of our life, after crossing which, we are ready to merge into the super consciousness, the Lord Almighty. The Lord Almighty also did full justice to these three stages, basics of life, when He bodily bound Himself in an incarnated form and through His deeds, His Leelas, His outward behaviour and paraphernalia He uplifted this entire creation towards the Light of the Lord. This He did in innumerable ways. After He took Mahasamadhi, His Samadhi is that core, that basis, which we have to ultimately reach but after crossing the three steps that depict life, i.e., we shed off the bodily digressions, crossing the very threshold of life, moving ahead on the spiritual path, to reach and attain unknown, undiscovered heights by holding onto the Light within or inside each one of us.

So if one has to attain the Lord, to merge into Him, for God alone knows how many lives, adorning peace and tranquility, then live this life to its fullest, as far as possible be "honest" to your own deeds, filling each incoming and outgoing breath with the Lord's name, then you will actually be justifying this human life, hence attaining it to the fullest, to merge into your Lord Sai. The Lord Almighty has given you this life to cross the three stages of life with Karmic elation and the Lord's name, to finally reach your destination, i.e., deliverance of the soul.

Baba's Samadhi in Shirdi is a true representation of this entire creation, the true identity of our life is concealed in this pious Samadhi. So the one who enters into the realms of this creation, the true identity of our life, innumerable sorrows which had to befall on us and many generations to follow will be easily cleared off, as its only then that we will merge into the Lord to attain Liberation. The feel of sorrow in our life keeps increasing or decreasing depending on our bodily digression or elation, but sorrow keeps fading away amid the power of the Lord's Name, that is why we humans will merge into the Lord Almighty after climbing the three steps of devotion to shed off sorrow.

If we try to see deeply, understand and experience this fact then each being basically lives two parallel lives—one of the body and the other of the soul. The former is a cause of pain, continuously moving towards death, i.e., its destruction or end is certain but the second one gives us joy and with the Lords Name as our bolster, on the seat of complete faith, full or saturated with love, is constantly moving towards the Lord's Divine Light. We humans, tied to the parameters of the body cry in sorrow, get dissuaded easily, hence adorning sorrow, restlessness, at times even lose our patience, while on the other hand, on the path of the soul we are only dependant on the Lord, fully relying on His Name, and keep distributing His Name, His treasure to the entire creation, which reaches us even amid innumerable difficulties, by His Grace. It is as though we get a feel of cool breeze even in the scorching heat of the sun. The satiation, the joy of this path is unparalleled, which may be swallowed up by the digression of the body for some time. The clouds may be dark and thick but can not hinder the sun from shining brightly.

Life is the "visible" form of the Lord and each step of the Samadhi signifies our progress in life, where the bodily self or sorrow in life keeps receding with each step and the Lord is clearly visible depicting the elation of the soul. Our body is continuously regressing yet on the threshold of truth, love, devotion, our soul is constantly progressing or being elated. Progress of the soul is assured if the steps of our life as arising from the base of the Samadhi, i.e., the basis of Crossing the threshold of life is our Guru God Sai—Constant chanting of the Lord's name. His name is actually a part of each incoming and outgoing breath.

Baba's Samadhi depicts a pious immortal life and hence each step towards this immorality, this purity will only lead us to shores beyond our perception and will ferry this soul to the undiscovered horizons for which this mortal coil is a mere means to cross the three stages of life, one step after the other. If we make Sai, His Name, His Samadhi the basis of the three stages of our life then the soul will be ferried safely to its origin,, i.e., the Lord where our body is like the boat that is carrying this soul, with the oar of Sai Naam, to His Samadhi. His Samadhi repeatedly tells us that before the final deliverance, before merging into the Ocean, i.e., the Lord Almighty, we have to live the life assigned to us, crossing all stages typical to a "life", undergoing all kinds of ups and downs, only then will causes be created to win over sorrow, to open new horizons for the divine flight of the soul. Only after crossing the three steps of life will the doors of unending happiness, joy, contentment open to us, the doors of the Samadhi of the Lord Almighty.

So Keep moving on the path of life with a pure and honest self, at each step dedicate all at the Lotus feet of the Lord with full Faith, so that we finally merge into the origin of our very being, i.e., attain the Lord Almighty.

So move on, step on (not physically) each step of the Samadhi and attain the true mission of your life, i.e., deliverance or liberation.

Baba had also said that, "though I will cast off this mortal coil but my Samadhi will talk and communicate with everyone, as I will be "ever alive" from My Samadhi." So Baba's Samadhi is a resting place for the physical aspect of the Para Brahma that incarnated on earth and it is also the foundation of the ever alive spiritual or Godly self of the Lord Almighty. Baba's Samadhi is actually HIS LIVE FORM and undoubtedly when we move close to the ever alive Sai, i.e., climb the steps of the Samadhi, then surely our sufferings will come to an end and hence Generations of sorrow and suffering shall cease.

As we move towards light, that darkness of life is lost, as we wake to a new morning, sleep of the night is gone, as we adorn now clothes that old ones are just shed off, as we fill our life with good deeds that negativity vanishes, as we chant the Lord's name that evil diminishes, as we believe in the power above and inside us that fear and doubt disintegrate, as we go to Shirdi and as we step on, admire and assimilate the three steps of the Samadhi that our sorrows are lost forever.

The speed of the car we drive is proportionate to the acceleration given and as we keep moving closer to the Lord greater will be our atimic elation, hence shedding off the digression of this body, we will merge into the Bliss of the soul.

The basic nature of the body is sorrow or pain, happiness or digression, to bear all kinds of turmoil but the soul is satiated with the Lords Name, to enhance towards the Lord. The parameters, limited threshold of the body can not touch the soul. They can only be a means to enhance the soul towards the super soul. So the closer we move to the Samadhi, we will automatically move away from sorrow or the bodily self will be shed off proportionately to the firmness of our faith and bodily sorrow will not regress us. Till we are in a body, difficulties are bound to surround us, but the Lords Name, His satiating peace giving feel, devotion, love and Grace of His feet will act like an armor, protecting us in the vicissitudes of life.

So the steps of the Samadhi are a direct ticket to the shores beyond, for Atmic elation, towards the Param Atman and bodily suffering automatically ends.

That is why:
"*Climbing the steps of the Samadhi*
Generations of sorrow and suffering shall cease."
So be it!
Om Sai Ram!

Third Promise

Even after I cast off this mortal coil. I will come running to the call of my devotees and for their benefit alone.

In this promise Baba has introduced us clearly to His Omnipresence, conveying that His being with His devotees is not dependant on, or a slave of a mortal coil. He merely adorned a mortal coil for fools like us, so that we can relate to Him easily, as we are bound to a mortal coil. In fact Baba is with us at all times, always, either as a bodily incarnated God or in His omnipresent form. The body is subject to decay, hence it will be cast off one day but the Lord God "always" comes running to any call of love from His devotees. No parameters of a body can bind "HIM" from reaching His devotees in any form or the way He desires.

As the light of the sun never diminishes or fades, it keeps spreading its radiance always, all around, any one being can not bind its light for oneself alone, no power can conceal it from reaching one and all, no power whatsoever can destroy it. The water in a river also paves its own path, filling the emptiness of waterfalls, ponds, lakes in this wonderful world, filling the emptiness that has been assigned by mother nature—only a form. A river fills this form or empty space with its pure water, replacing this emptiness with its flow, its pace. Similarly the Lord Almighty also gives life to this lifeless mortal coil. In fact the "life" in us is the Lord alone, who is filling our hollow lives with His form as the soul. As we cannot see or touch the soul, so we are unable to recognize, know or assimilate His true form. Hence to introduce us to our own true selves, to get us face to face with His divine self residing inside each one of us, the Lord incarnates on this earth, bound to a form. The incarnation of Lord Dattatreya appeared as "Sai Baba" in Shirdi. Living a simple life He created or played a number of Leelas or the apparent deeds and through these Leelas He granted us His true identity, in one way or another He introduced us to our true selves. He awakened His Divinity in the soul residing inside us that the strings of devotion started playing on the tune of love and surrender, each pore of our body was filled with divine joy, by the feel of His divine self which He showered through His miracles. Even though we are bound to this mortal coil, as human beings, yet His Grace gave us a feel that God is not only walking with us in a form as Sai Baba, but He is an integral and essential part of each speck inside, outside, all around us, in fact He is everywhere. This He did so beautifully through His Leelas that our inner self, that was asleep due to the dark cover of maya, had to awaken, had to wake up to His call of love and bathe in His Divine Grace.

Baba introduced us to this reality, He bound Himself in the bondages of a body so that He could give us His true glimpse. Yet while dwelling in this so called bondage of the body He, over and over again, introduced us to His unending, Omnipresent form that is spread everywhere, forever. This He did, so that once He leaves the mortal coil, to merge back into His unending self, to be once again alive in His omnipresence, He can be always visible to us through His Samadhi. When we are not able to see Him in His bodily form, His feel, His omnipresence always touches us, so that we are able to understand, know and imbibe this vast, unending self of Lord Sai. For example we see perfume enclosed in a glass bottle and occasionally when it is sprayed we get that scintillating smell as scent cannot be seen only felt and slowly we learn this fact, that to get a feel of this perfume in the bottle, we have to spray the same. Similarly the Godly self concealed in the Saintly glimpse of the Lord or Sai Baba is sprayed on us occasionally by the means of our devotion, love and surrender in His Lotus feet so that we get a feel of that "Divine perfume", we get the concealed Godly company.

In times to come, when there is no perfume left in the bottle or when the container is given away, i.e., when the Saintly form of the Lord is no longer visible, as it is the rule of any mortal coil-one that is created has to meet its end, still we are able to get a feel of the divine, a feel of the divine perfume even when the container is lost, as now the perfume bottle is empty. Now the perfume is there in the air, all around, always. It is by the power of His name that this is possible and its our surrender at His Lotus feet that grants us "His Grace". By adorning a mortal coil the Lord holds our hand and introduces us to His Divine radiance, which is actually always present in and around us. He grants us the feel of His concealed Divine self, so that when He leaves His mortal coil and merges back into His true omnipresent self then His Divine presence, the invisible yet indivisible self always stays with us. Its this assurance that Baba has granted us in this precious saying before shedding off the mortal coil that "Even after I cast off my mortal coil, I will come running to the call of my devotees and for their benefit alone."

After shedding off His Mortal coil, even today Baba is "ever alive" for His devotees, in fact for one and all and is till date playing His Leelas for our benefit and upliftment. Wherever and whenever a devotee calls Him, that He appears in one way or another, without any delay—always protecting His devotees. In fact after shedding off His mortal coil He is illuminating this entire creation in a more omnipresent, divine, formless self. That divinity which could never be concealed by the bondages of this mortal coil. He had adorned a coil to elevate, liberate, we mortal beings, who are always bound to things and happenings.

For Baba this body was only a cover of glass which was covering an ever illuminative light, like a burning candle. Even if this glass cover exists or is not there but the light from the candle will always illuminate everything, spreading far and wide. But we foolish mortal beings are not competent enough to assimilate the Divine light behind the glass cover even by arduous efforts. To give us a repeated feel of His

Divinity, to make His light reach us, come what may, He adorned a mortal coil. This He did to give us a feel that even while dwelling in a body its bondages never touched the Lord. Even while sitting is Shirdi He could tell us about each one's life story and when one called or calls Him with Love, He crosses seven seas to appear for His devotee, in seconds—either in visions, in dreams, by making us read some relevant portion from anywhere, through the words spoken by some other being, in the form of a picture or in any possible way, He so desires. He gives us a feel of His hidden, concealed arrival, basically for our benefit.

Baba also presented another fact here that a mortal coil that is born or appears, its end is inevitable but when the Lords incarnated form takes Samadhi then His omnipresent, ever alive form presents itself in a more obvious, illuminative way, spreading all over, showing or giving a feel of His presence in this entire creation. Air present in a balloon takes the form of the balloon but when the balloon bursts then the air present in it becomes a part of this entire atmosphere, spreading all over. So Baba's adorning and shedding of a mortal coil is only an outward show or play of Maya, merely to introduce us to His Divine self, through a mortal coil as we are bound to a mortal coil, while the Lord is "always" with us—inside us, outside us in fact in every speck of this Universe but when we call Him with love and from the depths of our heart, in times of sorrow, pain, happiness or elation, and we really are yearning to get His Divine glimpses, with a heart filled with loving devotion, then positively the Lord never disappoints us. At times He accepts the food offered to Him in the form of a fly and at times He inflicts intense pain on us in our dreams in order to free us from pain ordained in our real life. At times He even crosses closed doors to command us to mark Tripunda (three horizontal lines) on His forehead and at times He gives us His feel in the orange radiance of the setting sun. At times He wakes us with the melodious sound of a koel (singing bird) and at others He gives us His divine touch, in the blowing wind. We may or may not be able to

see Him but He surely grants us His feel, His divine touch, unparalleled joy of His presence, in one way or another. The Lord may appear in a form or He may grant us His feel beyond the bondages of the body, the feel that we all have been experiencing, since God alone knows how many births. The feel that God gives us is, that He surely appears to His devotees, on their call of love, when a devotees heart yearns for His divine glimpses or when we want to be liberated from our sorrow. He holds our hand and grants us His feel, His divine company, hence bathing us in joy, making us fearless and taking us to shores beyond, i.e., liberating us. In the divine flight of devotion, on the call of the yearning soul of His devotees, on the reverberating voice of pure pious love, the Lord comes running, He has been doing so always and will reach out, even beyond eternity. This is Baba's promise and He has always stood by it, so it is authentic and forever, infinitely. He will always, forever fulfill this promise too, as all others, only our call of devotion should be filled with Honesty, intentions should be pure, a yearning to attain the Lord filled completely with devotion and love.
So be it!
Om Sai Ram!

Fourth Promise

Have full faith in your heart and the Samadhi will fulfill all your wishes.

Baba's Samadhi is that core, that basis where the Lords incarnated bodily form rests and its from here that His ever alive form, His omnipresent feel, His indivisible divine light is being radiated. Baba's taking Mahasamadhi is only an outward bodily show, as He has always "been", He always "is" and always "will be" as He is an integral part of each speck of this creation and even beyond. Taking Mahasamadhi is only an act of adherence to the norms of nature, to show or depict the fact that every beginning only leads towards an end, it is assured, imperative but the incarnations never go, they are ever alive in their ever illuminative, in their unending divine self even after shedding off this mortal coil. Baba's Samadhi is pure, pious as it embraces the Lords omnipresent, unending reality in the form of His bodily incarnated mortal coil. In fact His Samadhi is the source of "all power" that is radiating divinity, granting love to everyone, all living entities, hence showing us the path of humanity and loving devotion.

In this promise Baba is not only introducing us to the pious feel of the Samadhi, hence introducing us to His Immortal reality, inherent in the Samadhi but is also guiding and reminding us to pay great attention towards the feelings of our mind, i.e., to keep our mind, our thoughts, clean and unblemished. He is repeatedly reminding us that we have to nurture and guide our mind constantly, our mind that is an off shoot of coming together of the body and the soul. We have to release this mind from the bondages of this world, soaking it in the Lord's love, keeping the "growing faith" in this mind ever firm, in fact, under "all circumstances" come what may we should not let our faith shake, not even waver.

Baba knew that in times to come His incarnated coil would merge into infinity spreading all over after Seemolanghan, i.e., crossing the border or casting off the mortal coil and we mortals, we humans who are bound to the body alone will be disappointed, dejected that Baba will no longer be with us once He takes Mahasamadhi. To save humanity from this narrow way of thinking, from the closed narrow inner thoughts, that Baba explained to us in this promise that His Samadhi itself will act as "His alive form" hence progressing us on the path of hope and faith. Even though Baba's bodily form will not be visible but His Samadhi will be like His visible form, enhancing and spreading the fragrance of love and faith—it will act like a magnet, which will pull innumerable broken, rusted iron filings towards itself, hence giving us a feel of the touch stone, i.e., Parasmani, to polish our devotion, love, surrender, and making our faith "firm" and unshakable like "Himself", i.e., Sai. To get a feel of, to understand, to adorn the authenticity of this unparalleled fact, we have to pay full attention towards our "mind" because its this mind alone that is vagrant and is easily dissuaded by the attraction of Maya, it completely loses its calm and balance, is blinded in the glare of materialism, hence completely going off from the right track, fully sinking in the darkness of Maya. If the mind is always imbalanced and fully drenched in Maya, then love, surrender, faith towards the Lord will never nurture. This mind will always be measuring everything on the scales of gain and loss, always yarning for material comforts, as the thoughts had arisen in Damu Anna's mind—for material gains. The desires that arise from our mind are only able to give us satiation which lasts for a limited time, as innumerable wishes arise once one has been fulfilled, a never ending package. In this rat race even if one or two of these desires are not fulfilled that we start complaining to God, instantaneously, i.e., our faith wavers with a slight blow of the Karmic axe and this "vagrant" mind starts questioning the very existence of the Lord. When our mind is deluded, unable to walk straight in faith then even after touching the pious Samadhi of the Lord, getting a feel of the joy that the touchstone gives and even after gaining the satiation of His Divine Grace, We mortal beings will not be able to understand, gather and assimilate the same. We will only keep gathering the instability and delirium of our own minds.

Baba has assured us that if we have "full faith" in our heart, then all our desires will be fulfilled by the Grace of the Samadhi. Even in the absence of faith our desires will be fulfilled, the Lords Divine color will glow but the dark cover of materialism will make our faith colourless, lifeless, will Vanish in just one blow and will deprive us from being able to recognise, gather the Grace of the Lord flowing towards us. On the other hand the one thirsting for spirituality, the one who years for the Lords love, His glimpse, wants to bathe in His Divine Grace—the faith of such a devotee will never waver, never lose the right direction basically and wholly because of the bolster of "HIS NAME". There is a ceaseless flow of the Lord's love flowing by His Grace from His Samadhi—to gather this flow of Divine honey we have to make sure our faith is firm, we have to build pathways that never waver, so that this ceaseless flow of Divinity, His Grace keeps flowing to us, without any hindrances. We have to build such a path of faith that even the strongest storms of Maya are unable to hinder the flow of this Divinity and we keep moving towards liberation with full firmness and no mayavi blockage is able to block the purity flowing from the Samadhi to our pure inner self. Baba's Samadhi is like the sun which is regularly, ceaselessly showering its light and energy on us, but its the crooked ways of our Karmic cycle, the entangling play of our mind, that give us a feel of either light or darkness, at different times depending on our Karmic state of mind. "Firm faith" is that basis, that state of our mind which does not let our faith waver even in darkness. This sun of "our faith" is ever illuminative though we might not be able to see it in the darkness of the night, be rest assured its not lost or has not vanished. We are unable to see it due to the dark night of our Karmic regression. The movement or rotation of the earth is like our Karmic cycle, yet the Lord or the Sun is always with us and soon this Sun will pierce the darkness of sorrow, once again spreading its light in the peace giving hue of the morning, filling our life with a new morning, a new beginning, hence bathing us in its joy. Unparalleled "Faith" is that firm conviction which assures us of the "light being concealed or hidden in darkness itself." The unshaken faith knows that soon light will pierce this darkness and shine, be visible, illuminate, will spread all around us as "our faith". Human nature is such that we mortals are easily lost in the intoxication of Maya, of comforts and become unstable when we are face to face with the darkness of sorrow. To be able to recognize the Lord, we have to be balanced in happiness and sorrow, i.e., all extremes of life, hence not letting our faith in the Lord waver, whatever the situation may be. Wherever there is "faith", Lords love and His Grace is flowing from His Samadhi from this very source, i.e., without any hindrance, without the interruptions or extremes of Maya. "Samadhi" itself is the visible form of the Lord, it is His Live presence and the waves arising from the same are solely for Human benefit or enhancement, making sure that each living being is being blessed by this Divine Grace of the Lord and so we all get a feel of His Divinity. If we always thank God in Happy times and keep our faith firm in sorrow, not doubting the very existence of God when in dumps, dedicating or giving up our all at His Lotus feet—happiness, sorrow, pain, joy, fear-fearlessness, with this firm conviction that He alone is the doer, we are merely puppets in His hand, then surely we will be filled with satiation, a sense of satisfaction in good times and will be able to see God with us in sorrow too. With the power of His name we will be developing a firm, unshaken faith, that this faith itself will cross the limited thresholds of "expectations" of this body, filling our entire life with the

Lords love, His Grace, spiritual enhancement, drenching our inner self with the unseen undreamt, unasked for, unalterable spiritual hopes and aspirations, on the threshold of "FAITH" alone. Our today is an outcome, off shoot of the Grace of the Lord flowing to us from His Samadhi, filling our inner self with pure, firm faith of His Divine Grace.

Hence always and forever:

"Have full faith, in your heart and the Samadhi or the Lord will fulfill all your wishes."

So be it!
Om Sai Ram!

Fifth Promise

Know that I am ever alive,
Experience and realise the truth.

Baba is omnipresent, an integral part of each living being, animate and inanimate objects, each feeling, every experience, in fact a part of every incoming and outgoing breath, in every beat of our heart. So His "not being" is impossible, this thought is merely a reason to delude oneself, an outward show of Maya to mislead us. Though we are familiar with and know this fact very well, yet we are deluded and wonder where is Baba? When will He come? When will He unfurl Himself for His devotees? This is so, maybe because we mortals are ourselves tied down by a mortal coil and when we are unable to understand the soul within, i.e., the Lords form inside each one, then it is really very difficult to gather or assimilate the all pervasive, ever alive, omnipresent, indivisible form of the Lord, that is an integral part of every speck of this creation. This promise, like all others, is also undoubtedly for our benefit alone as Baba knew that after His Mahasamadhi, once He is alive in His omnipresent form, we mortals bound to a body will try to search Him in the limited parameters of this body. To enhance us from this small way of thinking, Baba said that He is "ever alive", at times in a form, as Sai, and at others is Omnipresent—in every speck, each being, in me, in you, in fact everywhere. The day we understand this reality that we will be able to establish the true form of the Lord inside us, its the Lord alone who will smile in every living being, we will be able to see Him in every flower, leaf, animate or inanimate creation, its He alone who will reach us in every living or immovable form around us. Life and death are merely enactments of this body but the journey of this soul crosses many thresholds, after adorning many forms, to move towards its true mission, i.e., to be one with the Lord. The soul wants to be free from the bondages of this body and merge back into its indivisible true identity—like the Lord it wants to embrace omnipresence, as it is a part of the omnipresent Lord only.

We have to make an attempt to realise and attain the omnipresent, ever alive, indivisible form of the Lord, while dwelling in this body. We have to nurture it by the water of His Name, on the platform of firm faith in Him and Him alone. Slowly and steadily we have to shed off our bodily self, hence progressing towards the joy of the soul. We have to recognize, realize, attain the same, i.e., the Lord, hence losing our own self in His identity, to embrace Moksha, mukti, deliverance or liberation.

The authenticity of the promise, this vachan can be felt by everyone, each being, even today, as the experiences that devotees got while Baba was in a body, we can feel even today, after Baba's Mahasamadhi. Even today Baba comes running to the call of a devotee, the call may be from anywhere—from Shirdi itself or from across seven seas but His reply—different and unique in each case, is the one that pleases the Lord and annihilates the devotee. His shedding off the mortal coil does not hinder Him form reaching anyone, anywhere, anytime, as He is omnipresent. When Baba came to Shirdi bound to a mortal coil, He introduced one and all to His omnipresence—at times He spelt out someone's entire life story, at other times He conveyed His messages by appearing in dreams or visions, putting our doubting minds to rest by His words, "I do not need a door to enter anywhere". He gave us a feel of His Omnipresence many times, in fact over and over again by the medium of His teachings, precious sayings, visions and miracles. We got a feel of the Lord's omnipresent self, yet we mortals were always bound to His bodily form. We kept searching Baba only in the Dwarkamaayi, Chawadi, Lendi Bagh or rather just in the streets of Shirdi, till we did not prostrate before His bodily form (while Baba was in a bodily form), our doubting, vagrant mind was not at rest. When we mortals could not understand His Omnipresent form, while He revealed the same to us while He was in a body, then after His shedding off the mortal coil, i.e., after Mahasamadhi, we mortals try to find Him only in the Samadhi Mandir and bow to His form there. To get a glimpse of the Lord we again and again become a part of the long que leading to the Samadhi Mandir, for hours together, yearning, hoping to get His pious Divine glimpse...At times we sing and at others cry to call Him, at times we wake Him and at others put Him to sleep. There is no doubt that the Lord's bodily form is a picture of His indivisible identity, as its here that the seed of the thought process of, we mortals rests, i.e., we have to attain the indivisible, unseen Lord by holding the hand of His "visible" form. We have to know and attain the Brahmand within from the path that originates from Shirdi in Maharashtra, i.e., we have to attain the Shirdi within, we have to engrave, attain, invoke, illuminate the omnipresent, ever alive, indivisible form of the Lord within. Maybe then His pious feel arises inside us and instead of repeating these words over and over again—Baba when will you come? When will you embrace us? When will you hold our hand? When will you make us sit in your lap? We mortals have to realize this fact that Sai is not separate from us, He is in and around us, in fact everywhere and anywhere. There is no speck in this universe which is not filled with Sai. Only when we understand this, that we will realize that we are not separate from Him, He is always with us, in fact He alone is always with us, He is our true identity, every experience in life is Him and He alone is the source of our breath—the soul inside us, His "live" form within us.

"Know that I am ever alive"—this fact tells us that the limited parameters of the body cannot bind the Lord, His being with His devotees is not a slave of a mortal coil. He is with "All" His devotees at the same time—blessing some through visions and to some other's He appears in their sleep, to some He flows through the ambrosia of the Pothi, yet others get His feel in each breath they take. Always be sure and hold onto this fact firmly that Baba is with everyone, all the time, at every step, everywhere, but we fools, tied to the bondages of this body made of five elements, blinded by the intoxication of Maya are unable to see, understand or get a true "feel" of Him. Like the deer we keep wandering in search of the Kasturi that is concealed inside us. By the power of His Name, with His Divine Grace, the day we get a feel of His Divine Grace at all times, everywhere, always—while eating, sleeping moving or doing anything, we realize His presence with us "Always" and instead of calling Him again and again we know that He is Always with us, then He alone becomes an indivisible part of our life, when He alone is seen and felt everywhere, in everything, in and around us. This means we are on the right track of self realization. When we eat we offer the same to Him who is dwelling inside us, if we are in any dilemma then we should always talk to Him only and always chant His name, to receive His reply immediately and instantaneously. We can feel the joy of His voice in the melodious song of the koel (a melodious bird), His touch can be felt by us in the soothing feel of the breeze, His form alone shines for us in the illuminating sun, whatever text we read its Sai alone who shines as the basis of all that is read, sing any song, even if they are from films, be elated by connecting all with Him, while cooking get a feel that He is helping you do the same standing right next to you. Whenever tired feel as though He alone is patting you with love, if someone fights, understand that Sai is teaching you a lesson to be patient, if someone showers love towards you realise that Sai is pouring His Ocean of Grace on you, it may be a friend or a foe, each one is teaching you something new, as though a representative or messenger of Sai. With the power of His name alone He fills our vision, our entire self with His identity in such a way that the wide creation seems to take His form. This is not impossible, but it takes time to climb the steps of progress, so be patient, as here too Baba is teaching us a lesson of patience.

With passage of time, with every feel, with every experience in life we get familiar with His Omnipresent form, So the question of His not being with us after His Mahasamadhi does not arise. He is with everyone and for the protection of one and all, we can rely only on Him. He can save a frog from the mouth of death, can sleep on a small wooden plank hung to the rafters with torn pieces of cloth, with earthen lamps burning all night on its four sides, gives Udi to some when they need it during a journey, and puts to rest the pain during child birth with this amazing Udi. Even while dwelling in a body He introduces us to His omnipresent form, over and over again and now He is ever illuminative in His omnipresent form in this entire creation. The scintillating glow arising from the Divine Sun—His Samadhi—is illuminating this entire creation. One may be in any corner of the world but Baba shows His Divine Glimpse to one and all—by appearing to His devotees in innumerable ways, He satiates them. His ways of working are varied and wide spread that it is impossible to gather or understand them fully. As we cannot trap air, can not bind the very identity of the sun, we can only get a feel or experience the same. So is the Divinity of the "Divine Master". By understanding this omnipresent feel of the Lord we have to keep moving on the path of life, towards the Lord, at every step, every experience, all around, get His feel always with us, as the Lord is nothing but "self experience". So each one of us has to know this truth, with His Divine Grace alone, that we have to attain our true identity, in and through His "ever alive" form, losing our bodily self to the Divine, indivisible identity of the Lord, only then will we be able to understand, realize and assimilate the fact that the Lord is "ever alive". We have to attain our true selves in the Divine joy by assimilating and imbibing the innumerable experiences showered on us, by Him, so that we can move on the path of deliverance and ultimately attain "GOD".

Baba always was, He is with us today and He will always be with us—this reality we have to understand, assimilate and attain solely with His Grace and with the power of His name—The reality being—"Know that I am eve alive"—we have to ourselves experience the same and have to recognize and attain this indivisible fact of life.

So be it!

Om Sai Ram!

Sixth Promise

Show unto me he who has sought refuge and has been turned away.

Human life represents good fortune as its only in this life that we can attain our destination, on the consorts of Karma and Bhakti or devotion, we can adorn salvation by embracing the divine form of the Lord, that is why all creation, right from God to demigods to demons are eager to get a human life as its this life alone which grants us salvation, liberation. As humans, while performing our deeds, filled with true love, with a heart full of devotion, we can attain our true destination, i.e., adorn the Lord, hence filling our own self with divinity, to get rid of the cycles of birth-death-rebirth, i.e., attain moksha or liberation. But in the clever play of Maya, in its hollow, intoxicating artificiality, we tend to lose the right direction in life, hence using this mortal coil only in its luxuries, laziness and negativity while it was assigned to us basically to merge into the Lord to be one with Him. We do remember and worship the Lord but only for our bodily comforts, to attain missions only initiated and directed by Maya. We are hence deprived of the true divinity, the real essence of the Lord, His Divine Grace, losing ourselves and aimlessly wandering in the darkness of Maya.

To put, we mortals, on the path of our true mission, to make our human life worthwhile, the Lord Himself incarnates on this earth to show us this true path which we have forgotten. The Lord Himself gives a tap to our dormant inner self, He awakens our true inner self, He introduces, we mortals, to His Divine self while adorning a body, so that the dormant strings of devotion play to His Divine tune and the

Divine light is seen and felt by us, that light which reaches us after piercing the dark covering of Maya, its peace giving and elating feel helps us progress on the spiritual path, i.e., shows us the right path of elation, so that we mortal beings, who are sleeping in the tyring sleep of Maya, should wake up and after drenching in the Lords Grace, we should bathe in the true joy of the Lord. We should be able to see and understand this fact that the Lord makes tremendous effort and adopts innumerable ways to reach us and inspires us to sit in the cool shade of His Divine Grace. He repeatedly gives us this feel, shows us this reality that He is ever eager to embrace us with open arms, He is eager to fill the devotee with Divine Joy. Probably God is more eager than us to take us under His secure wing, to embrace us in His Loving embrace. Who are we to call Him? We are incapable of asking Him for anything. We in fact are not competent to even express our sorrow to Him, how can we exhort the inner feelings of our heart to Him as we are unable to even understand His indivisible presence inside us, as the soul. On the other hand He is "Knowledge itself", He alone knows the lives we have lived from one form to another. He knows us in and out, that is why He creates such circumstances over and over again for us to be able to sit in His loving lap, so that we mortals, who are walking on burning ember of life should get a sign of relief and hence bathe in the Lords Divine grace by moving on the path of deliverance to finally embrace our true destination, i.e., liberation and ultimately merge in peace.

Baba repeatedly gives or grants us such opportunities in life so that we can turn our life towards the Lord even while sitting in the mire of materialism or amid the Karmic cycle. When we are tormented by pain, its only then that we are reminded of the Lord and in the happier times of life we want to always thank the Lord for His Grace as that is what gives us peace and satiation. Its human nature that—"We always worship the Lord when in sorrow and tend to forget Him in times of happiness"—maybe that is why due to bodily regression, as a result of misdeeds that we face sorrow in life. A human being who is suffering immensely, bodily, due to his Karmic cycle, calls the Lord from the depths of the heart whereas in the intoxication of joy we tend to forget the Lord and are lost in joy, hence assigning our own selves, the position of a doer, forgetting the real doer (God). To repeatedly remind us of His being with us always, to turn our entire self towards the Lord at all times in life, happy or sad, and to fructify this feeling of His Divine Presence, Baba over and over, in all situations gives us His true feel and shows us that path which leads us to His pious, peace giving, protective embrace, in happiness and in sorrow. He makes us chant His name totally based on His Grace, so that we mortals who have been sent on this earth to get deliverance, should not be buried under the filth of Maya, hence losing ourselves to its darkness. In fact we should get a place in the Lap of His Incarnated form, on the threshold of His Name, to progress towards "Light" and hence attain the true mission of life.

This was the glory of the Lord's name—in happiness and sorrow, but the Lord does not want to bind us in material happiness or sorrow, or in the give and take of any kind when He gives us place in His lap. He wants to give us a caress of love, wants to enhance us on the path of devotion, to give us a glimpse of the divine horizon in His pious home of spirituality. He has appeared to pull us out from the digression of Maya and enhance us towards the direction of His Divine Light—our true Mission. Its we foolish mortals who do not leave the thread that binds us to materialism. We don't give up our inherent nature of greed even after going to the Lord's abode and even after getting the good fortune of sitting in His pious lap. Only the rat race of Maya pleases us. Even under the Lord's protective embrace we yearn for name, fame, the jingling sound of coins. Its solely because of our materialistic mind set and inclination that the Lord says that His lap lies vacant to receive His true disciple. While sitting in the Lord's lap if we yearn only for Maya, we would probably get the same, fully depriving ourselves of the devotional grace filled with love that is constantly flowing from Him for our benefit. We will be left assimilating mere materialism in this mortal coil. The layers of Maya surrounding us will not let the Divine touch of the Lord reach us—the Grace that the Lord is eager to shower on us. This veil of Maya will not let the strings of our inner self play the tune of true devotional love.

Baba has said in the Sai Sat Charita that "people come to me like pots that have been placed upside down",, i.e., we are unable to imbibe what He really wants to grant us. We do not become the true recipients of His Grace, as the flow of His devotion, the unparalleled joy of His Grace is lost and flows from the outside—hence is unable to even touch us. We only keep gathering Maya in this material pot, i.e., our mortal coil, those material objects and things that will just flow away or will be lost one day, try as hard as we may, we will never be able to assimilate this Maya forever. It will be lost, just like the flow of this life.

We go to the temple, in Baba's loving embrace, ask for materialism and achieve the same but even if a single wish is left unfulfilled that we start complaining and call the Lord over and over again. We are unable to understand this reality that if we ask for things that are not going to last even a life time then how will we even gather the omnipotent? We are restricted to only the slave of the Lord's feet, i.e., Maya, then how will we ever get a chance to sit in His lap, gathering unparalleled fortune beset with divinity? The ones who desire materialism are the worshippers of Laksmi alone but the ones who yearn for spirituality are able to reach the Lords protective embrace in the true sense, hence embracing the Divine light of devotion and love. The ones asking for materialism, of name, Maya, only perform bodily actions hence entangling fully in the web of Karmas. Real joy of the Lords Grace is only a dream for them. We are granted the Divine Grace of God, only if we yearn to attain the Lord, worship Him with purity of heart, struggle to attain Him, even amid Maya. Its only then that we are filled with HIS unbroken Divine Light, filling us with love and devotion, taking us up to the doorstep of deliverance, we are able to surrender our life fully at His Lotus feet, truly and sincerely, hence making our life worthwhile—worth living.

We mortals are mere puppets in the hands of Maya—we are born of maya, its maya that sustains us, we are deluded in one way or another by maya and we only yearn for the same in innumerable ways. We do worship the Lord but our thirst for maya is ever alive. We go to the temple, worship Him but desires that surface are only material. That is why Sai Baba says, "My lap, my pious embrace is lying empty" (meri sharan aa khali jaaye). The one who crosses the horizons of this body, while bodily dwelling in the same in the true sense merges in the Lord's embrace, finds a place in His lap. Such a one is desirous only of "HIS" Divine grace, wants to merge or lose his or her identity in the Lord alone because such a one loves only the master of this body even while being bound by the materialism of this body.

Further Baba has said, "Just reach me with open arms or tell me your needs, i.e., true needs of the soul." Those mortals who do not desire only materialism but yearn to be "one" with the Lord, want to move on the spiritual path with honesty and sincerity—such beings should "call" the Lord with an honest intent and pure self. It is not possible that the Lords Grace would not flow to such a one. The inner self of such a one will bathe in Divine Bliss and will surely attain the "desired" destination. Baba has also said the same in the Sai Sat Charita that good thoughts always bear fruit by His Grace alone. Next time you go to the Lord's abode, i.e., a temple, and spread your hands in front of Him, at this juncture search and ask your own inner self that are you remembering the Lord only for material ends or its the yearning for His love that is the basis of your life? With such thoughts in the mind, all complaints, bickerings will vanish, desires will just crumble such as whether the Lord gave us something or not, as the one who has gone under His protection, the one rapt in His love and devotion can never remain empty handed. With His arms wide open the Lord is repeatedly showing you the true destination, i.e., His loving embrace, His lap is still empty—waiting to embrace the true worshipper of "love" and "love" alone. The true gain of our life is His love and we should be ever ready to receive the same—His love alone. This is what Sai is repeating in this promise and calling us with open arms to grant us His loving embrace.

Om Sai Ram!

Seventh Promise

As are your feelings towards me,
So is the colour of 'My' inner self

Its our true inner feelings that can ferry us across this Ocean of Mundane Existence. If our thoughts, our feelings are good then the off shoots of our Karmic cycle will also be visibly good, pleasing to our mind. If our inner self is filled with malice, hatred then even outwardly exhibited good behaviour or sweet words will not fill our life with sweetness. On the other hand if our inner self is healthy, under all circumstances, filled with purity and honesty, devoid of partiality, distributing happiness to one and all then even the prick of thorns, i.e., tough times in our life will also seem like the flow of our Karmic gives and takes and we will win over this struggle of life in this pious flow, hence the negatives in life will not regress us further.

This mortal coil is made of mainly five elements of nature and will be shed off after undergoing the plus and minuses of life, gaining a higher strata or regressing to a lower life form according to its Karmic elation or digression. The soul inside each one of us is a part of the "super soul"—it has moved away from its identity to finally merge into the same but the ups and downs of bodily Karmas make this soul spin in the cycle of 84 lakh life forms, i.e., it moves from one form to the other, changes its body yet remains unchanged. Our body signifies nature and the life in this bondage of nature is the soul, a part of the Lord. Then what is the mind? From where has it originated? This mind turns our body, a body created by the coming together of nature and God, i.e., body and the soul, towards devotion—it pushes us towards our true aim and at times takes us away from the same, i.e., dissuades us. We perform many Karmas by making this body a means and come what may we have to face the plus and minuses or effects created by our Karmas. These effects are borne by this mortal coil. On the other hand the veil in our mind, in our thoughts, hidden in our inner self as bad thoughts for others or in the form a cheating mind, are fatal. Its a common saying that outer, i.e., bodily wounds sooner or later are filled up, even if they leave scars, but wounds inside our body, i.e., the ill done by our mind—our thoughts prove to be fatal. The true mission of human life is to keep chanting the Lords name outwardly, by making this body a means, and gradually merge into the entire creation which is inside each one of us. If our mind is not pure and is always inclined towards bad thoughts, ill feelings then how will goodness find a place here? So first and foremost the purity of our mind is most important, it is pivotal.

Slowly, with the passage of time when the purity inside each one of us awakens, then it starts becoming a part of our intellect, our personality, soon spreading all over and all around us. So its the feelings inside us, i.e., in our mind that actually shape our personality and its our intellect that guides us into good or bad deeds, i.e., the path of our life is paved. That is why Baba used to say, "As are your feelings towards me, so is the colour of "My" inner self."

This entire creation is the Lord's abode as He is Omnipresent. So if we move on the path of life with a clean and pure inner self then we will surely be recipients of the same feeling from the innumerable forms of the Lord, i.e., other beings. So its the feelings of our mind that pave our Karmic cycle and its these deeds that either reward or punish us, as we sow so shall we reap. If we move on the path of life with pure, unblemished intentions then despite difficulties in life the Lord will always be with us, with the same honesty of intent that has been felt and experienced from the depths of the heart. His Grace is showered on us in accordance with the good or bad thoughts inherent in our mind.

Secondly, the Lord God dwells inside each one of us. Its He who is inside us, as the soul—the light, unending, unborn, indivisible self. So when we are "alive" as a result of His being in us, that the Lord God dwelling inside us is coloured in the same colour as our mind, our inner self, our inner thoughts. When He alone resides in us then how can He stay aloof from the mind inside us. We may be doing nothing outwardly but the minute any thought arises in our mind it immediately is relayed to the Lord within, i.e., the Lord God is fully in touch and knows all the thoughts that arise in our minds. For example, when our brain gives any order, our outer bodily self puts the same into action. Same way when waves arise in our mind, good or bad, then first and foremost their touch is felt by the identity of the Lord inside each one of us. In a nutshell we cannot conceal anything from the Lord as He dwells inside us. We may not put all thoughts into action but these good or bad thoughts are instantaneously registered in the Lord's account—a cause, i.e., Karma has been created for us to face its effect in times to come.

As new clothes cannot satisfy the pangs of hunger, only morsels of food are needed for satiation, similarly its our good deeds, positive thoughts, yearning to attain the Lord alone that give us a glimpse of the Lord, get the yearning soul face to face with the super soul. On the other hand cheating, dishonesty, negativity, bad deeds take us to the mire of regression, covering the Lord's identity in us, i.e., the soul with a thicker layer of the dirt of maya. The message that Baba gave to one and all while He bodily lived in Shirdi for 60 years and even today when He speaks from His Samadhi, running to the call of every devotee, He is still telling us that mere outwardly, bodily performed actions are not enough but He is fully and wholly driven towards the purity of mind, pure intentions, goodness, honesty, love and egoless surrender at His Lotus feet—its these good thoughts and deeds that please or appease Him. He accepts even a leaf offered with love but He lets go even gold, if offered with pride. This is the reason that at times Baba's face radiates love and divinity even while adorning simple cotton clothes and on the other hand dresses woven with the thread of gold and decorated with diamonds and pearls also seem colourless or without any radiance. So its the purity of our heart, i.e., your inner feelings that please the Lord whereas outward paraphernalia, pomp and show dissuade our own selves, then how can they please "GOD". Whenever, whosoever went to Shirdi got a glimpse of Lord Sai in the same form, that one was carrying in the casket of one's heart, i.e., according to our own feelings His Grace was poured on us. Worshippers of Lord Rama got His glimpse in Sai, while someone else perceived "HIM" as Gholap Swami, to some one Baba gave the order to draw a "tripunda", i.e., three horizontal lines, to enhance his devotion in Lord Shiva while some others were blessed with the rays, the radiance of miracles. Those thirsting for devotion bathed in His love while those desirous of material goods filled their bags with His unlimited grace, of the same. Those who wanted "proofs" of His omnipresence gathered miracles but those who surrendered fully at His Lotus feet were filled with His "Loving Devotion". If one desired to have butter milk the same was granted and if the mind got vagrant to attain materialism that Baba poured the Ganges of knowledge to save us, teaching us the efficacy of patience in His own Divine way. As were our desires so was His Grace. Some gathered flowers, leaves, prasad etc., and carried the same while some bathed in the Ganges of love and devotion flowing from one's own eyes—as were our feelings, so was the fruit that we got. Probably that is why Baba has said in the Sai Sat Charita that, "there will be no dearth of food or clothes in the homes of my devotees, if at all you have to ask for anything then ask for the Lord." Our inner feelings should be aimed towards attaining "the Lord", keeping our mind rapt in gaining His Divine Glimpse. Cry only because you are away from Him (apparently, outwardly), keep paving the path "only" to "reach HIM" with the stepping stones of "His Name", i.e., always chanting His name. If we repeatedly keep chanting His name then He will not be able to stay away from us for too long and He will surely grant us the fortune of HIS DIVINE form. On the repeated chanting of His name, He will not keep His true self concealed for too long, leaving you to suffer in the hands of Maya. On the call of His "name" repeated chanting of the same, He will surely merge "you" into His true divine self, breaking all barricades, all hindrances, the artificial veil of Maya. He will surely reach you, to build what you desire, make that reality the aim of your life which pleases and satisfies your inner self. To construct a house, building material is what one needs, one engulfed by worldly desires will be attracted by outward distractions, a desire for fame will probably get you to the level of an animal, a flood of never ending desires will trap you in a whirlpool of Maya. A hope to attain the Lord, a yearning to merge into His Divine form, a deep desire to get His Divine glimpse, the feel of His presence in each being will lead you to an end of duality, i.e., a sense of yours and mine will vanish by the power of the Lord's name leading you to the true identity of our human form, i.e., life itself, hence making this life worthwhile. The Lords Grace will elevate you from the mire of Maya and introduce you to the true form of the Lord. That is why it has been repeatedly stated that "Lord is in the hands of His devotees"—in fact He is bound to their love, devotion and surrender. As is the colour of unblemished pure love, so is the devotion awakened and its then that the Lord comes running to the devotee, filling the devotees love towards Him with His Divine Grace, unending love, putting a devotees devotion on the right path of the Lord, granting him Lord's glimpse even while he is in a mortal coil. Love is a synonym of God. So His Divine appearance is directly proportional to the purity of our love towards Him. The yearning of our heart to be one with Him is the bell of the temple that resounds inside each one of us, its the thread of love which binds the Lord to reach His devotee, filling the devotee with Divine Bliss and hence enhancing him towards the Lords divine grace, making him the proud recipient of the Lords Grace, peace, contentment and elation.

Our mind has been created in such a way that it is very easily influenced by Maya, hence losing itself in the darkness of the same, wavers from its path, hence losing the true vision. But it has been rightly said by a poet, "open the eyes of your mind and you will get your beloved", i.e., fill your inner self with the Lord's name and His Love, flood of His name, i.e., constant chanting so that it gets impossible for Maya to stay there for too long. Even though Maya is eager to dissuade you, do show it the face of failure by the power of your love towards the Lord. Only then will the inner eyes open, i.e., the spiritual path will be visibly wide, clearer and then we will surely meet the beloved—our Lord Almighty. He will glitter like the Golden Sun inside you after washing the dirt of Maya, engulfing your mind, with the water of His Name. He will radiate His divinity all around, through you. So its our mind that is bound by the chains of Maya. We have to open the same by the key of the Lord's name, for the minds liberation. We have to fill our mind with an earnest desire to be "one" with the Lord; making it soar to unseen, untouched horizons. When the mind is "pure" then the pious Ganges of love and devotion will ceaselessly flow from within.

So, "As are the feeling of our inner self, so is the colour of the Lord's inner self."

Baba's promise here enhances us towards the development of a pure pious inner self. It shows us the path, where we can shed off outer artificiality and be adorned by the beauty of a pious inner self. The outer paraphernalia may not be very pleasing or attractive but we have to illuminate our inner self, i.e., our mind with HIS NAME, making it move on the threshold of hope, to be one with the Lord so that it ultimately merges into the Lord and hence rests in peace. We have to develop and create such a pure pious self inside each one of us, that Lord Sai shines from within. If the feelings, the names originating from our inner self are filled with "SAI" then there will be synchronisation of inner purity with outer chanting. The true form of the Lord will be awakened inside us, will flow in all directions, all over from our inner self, introducing us to its omnipresent self, hence rewarding us with its true Divine form. So if you have to attain the Lord, you want to bathe in HIS DIVINE BLISS then cleanse your inner self with the pure water of His Name, lay out the seat of love for Him to sit on, wave the fan of devotion and find, discover, revere and worship the Incomparable, indivisible Lord Sai seated here—"Inside You".

Om Sai Ram!

Eighth Promise

All your Burden I will bear.
This promise will be ever true.

Each word spoken by our "Lord Sai" is the word of Lord Brahma, i.e., "Brahma Vakya" and we all know that Lord Brahma is the creator of this entire creation and it is believed that whatever the Lord once writes in the book of our life, our destiny, it cannot be reverted even by the Lord Himself. So whatever Lord Sai did or said while He was in a mortal coil were nothing else but the Lord's words, i.e., His Creation. In fact these words were, are and undoubtedly will always remain the true reality of our life, there is no place for doubt, at all.

On every step, on the path of life, whenever we call the Lord, He always replies to each call in a different way, either from the place of worship, through another being, any event on the path of Karma or in the regular course of our life. His own special way of showing us the right path is actually our destiny or a tap to turn us towards our life's goal that we could see, understand and assimilate the path shown to us by the Lord. Our life progresses on the threshold of the Lords words, creations and directions and we keep progressing on the path shown by Him in accordance with Lord Brahma's Creation. We mortals keep facing joy, sorrow, happiness, depression, elation, digression on this Karmic path of life. At times we drown in sorrow and yet at other times we bathe in joy, yet life keeps moving on amid innumerable extremes. We tend to lose our balance in times of joy, elation, bliss as its intoxication fills us with ego and we design ourselves as "creators" but in sorrow we seem to come to a stand still, we are unable to bear the weight of digression, darkness. Its at this juncture, i.e., in times of sorrow that we cry and call the Lord, we go to the Lord's abode, may be a temple, or a mosque, to become fearless and free of our sorrows. The Lord comes running to every call of His devotees, the call of pain or sorrow, protecting us, by making us adorn HIS protective cover, the cover of His name and shows us the path of devotional love even in sorrow. This goes on life long or in fact life after life. At times we mortals fill ourselves with the Lord's Grace in times of sorrow and at others we take a flight into the unknown horizons of spirituality.

The Lord may turn the direction of our life towards good deeds as Rama, Krishna or Sai or in any other incarnated form by bearing the weight of Karmic engulfment of our lives on His shoulders. He would also send His messages to us in His unique amazing omnipresent way, to give us a feel of His true self. He would carry us from the mire of sorrow to make us reach the unknown, unimaginable heights of joy, of bliss. But this fact always came forth, pleased our mind, became the reason of our contentment, of our smile, in every situation, under all circumstances or in any way when we have been granted the "Lord's Grace". Every vicissitude of our life was borne by the Lord Himself, adorned by Him, but outwardly we felt it was the flow of our own Karmic cycle.

To cite an example when we drive a vehicle then outwardly, apparently and obviously we feel that we are driving whereas we are actually only using the different parts of a machine in an organised and controlled manner, that the vehicle is put into motion. Actually the machine parts, fuel, etc., are the cause of movement in the car. Similarly this body outwardly seems to be bearing the joys and sorrows of this life, which is merely an intoxication of Maya, a false image formed, as whatever we are performing outwardly is fully awakened and controlled by our inner self. Outer actions are of our body but the control is from within, similarly this body seems to be undergoing the pain and elation caused by sorrow and joy respectively but its true weight or effect is borne by the Lord, the "soul" inside each one of us. If this body signifies pain then the Lord is the ointment, if body is regression then the Lord is the only reason for our elation; if this body makes us fall down to dumps then its Sai alone who carries us out of these dumps, bearing the weight of all our Karmic effects, to ferry us to shores beyond our perception or reach. The Lord, merely by His loving touch, makes this mortal coil, that is constantly by reeling in the fear of death, capable of taking the spiritual take off, the ultimate flight, the real plunge.

We mortals are actually mere puppets in the hands of the Lord Almighty, the thread of our life is in His Divine hands. He makes us move, makes us dance to His tune, in life—as He feels like, whenever and whichever form but we are unable to see this invisible thread that controls us fully. On the other hand we feel that our thoughts, behaviour, deeds, reasons for our deeds are an off shoot of our own Karmas, actions, reactions, hence we deter or digress towards the darkness of Maya.

Our life is a creation, a result of the unification of Nature, our body and the Lord, i.e., the soul. As the soul enters this lifeless body as life that a new form is created, i.e., our mind which fully entangles and dissuades us in the entanglements of the body, hence regressing our growth towards the soul. We are totally bound by this body which is rapt in Karmas that give rise to desires, unsteadiness of mind, worries, incorrect thinking. We feel that each deed we perform is progressing us in life hence moving us towards the Lord, to attain our desired and ultimate destination, i.e., all our Karmas are taking us in the right direction. There is no doubt about this fact that Life is based on Karmas, Akarmanyata or not performing ones duty only regresses us to darkness, to be perished. It is impossible to stay without performing Karmas till the last breath. Its our deeds alone that generate the direction of our life. Good deeds alone turn us towards goodness. Its the actions performed in life alone that pave their reactions, i.e., Karmas generate the fruit we get—this is undoubtedly true, but for which Karma we will be rewarded or punished in which life is fully ordained by and in the hands of the creator—our Lord Almighty. We can make an attempt to beautify our life on the platform of Karma and bhakti but the tree that has been generated by the seeds of karma—when will it bear fruit and in what form is fully in the hands of the Lord alone. When and which deed will be performed by us, how and when will we move towards goodness or on the wrong path, will we be rapt in devotion and will be deeply in tune with the Lord or will we adorn the perishing path of jealousy—all is ordained by the Lord. We are merely performing our part like the different characters in a play, as a result of the intoxicating effect of Maya, this mortal coil and materialism. We are deluded and hence rejoice in all we do as our own creation.

Everything, may it be any work, deed, devotion, love, surrender—all is under the Lords supervision, under His control, that is why Baba has said—"I will bear all your burden. My promise will never be false". When He alone is the doer of all deeds, Lord alone is the deed performed and He alone bears the effects of these actions—its He alone and no one else, then why should we fear? Undoubtedly He alone is bearing the weight of the bodily deeds, has always borne it for us and will bear the same, always. So whatever duties "He" alone has assigned to us on this path of life, we should perform them with full dedication, with a pure honest self, yet not getting or developing a feel of doership within ourselves, instead dedicate all actions of this body and mind at His Lotus feet. Then may it be your body or the mind, Karmas may give you sorrow or digression why should you feel the weight of the same as you are merely a means? In reality and totality its the Lord alone who has taken the weight of all our burdens on Himself—we seem to be carrying it only outwardly, bodily. Know and realize the fact, the assurance or promise made by Sai Baba and be ever free of all your burdens and live a simple life devoid of all cleverness, filled with devotional love. He will give you a feel of being free of your so called burdens, He will enhance it for you so beautifully that you will not be aware of this fact. Never ever give up love, faith, dedication and honesty of thought, word and action towards Him and everything in life and keep moving humbly on this path of life by making and taking "HIS WORDS" as the very basis of your life—as the true identity of your life. Then even while carrying the weight of this body you will be able to enjoy the weightlessness, the divine flight of the soul. Even though pressed down by the weight of your own Karmas, you will be able to take the flight of deliverance, finally merging in the embrace of the Lord—you will be one with HIM, i.e., attain the true mission of this human life.

So be it!
Om Sai Ram!

Ninth Promise

*Come take all the help you desire, as what
you have asked for is not too far.*

Human nature is such that we mortals are running endlessly to fulfil our never ending desires. In this madness to fulfil our desires, we knowingly or unknowingly are engulfing ourselves in a cycle of both good and bad deeds, hence creating a Karmic web around us, spun with the threads of our never ending desires. The Lords Name, His grace, slowly, one by one cuts these threads of our Karmic web. Even while dwelling in this body it grants us a feel of being free, being liberated, grants us the feel of the Lord, smiles as "light" in our lives even amid darkness, hence ferrying us across to shores beyond this mundane life.

We mortals perform Karmas all our life and the irony of this Karmic cycle is such that if its fruit grants us goodness, praise, a comfortable life that we are fully intoxicated by its effect, hence taking our own selves to be the real doers, which turns the face of our life, automatically towards the darkness of life. On the other hand if we have to suffer pain due to the ill effects of our Karmas and as a result of the same we are granted sorrow, restlessness, its then that we put all the burden of the same on the Lord's head, blaming Him for our digression, sorrow, pain. When goodness and comforts came forth then it is our deeds that bore fruit and when pain and sorrow surround us, that we halt at that point wondering, is this what our Lord has given us, why? Yet the Lord is very merciful that despite our selfish way of thinking He still saves and protects us from our own digressive thoughts, either by taking our sorrow on His own self hence making us free of the same or by giving us the power to bear our sorrow, solely due to His Grace. By pulling us out of our pain and darkness and by putting us on the true, the real path of spirituality, over and over again. His effort to put us on the right track goes on endlessly.

Our mortal coil has been created due to the unification of five elements of nature, though life is instilled in this lifeless form by the Param Atman in the form of the atman but this body is a unification of the elements of nature so it is natural that we mortals are only bound to our body, as we can see and feel the same. We are always rapt in gathering comforts, adornments only for this body or are busy in satiating the endless desires generating from our mind, forgetting that this mortal coil was created by the Lord for "His own" stay, as atman, so that we could strive, reach and realize the soul inside us by making this body a means. But we foolish mortals keep spinning between the two parts of Maya, i.e., our body and the mind. We keep ourselves busy in fulfilling the endless desires of our mind, forgetting that we had to generate such Karmic vibrations so that the path of our life is turned towards attaining the form of the Lord, dwelling inside each one of us. We mortals are fully blinded by the cover of Maya, hence, we keep striving for comforts and happiness, all our life. For the sake of this perishable mortal coil we forget humanity and lose the humane touch. Come what may, our deeds may be good or bad but we mortals make all possible attempts to fulfil our desires and in this horrendous pace, passionate desires, we plant the seed of misdeeds, knowingly or unknowingly—our life is tied between the two ends of the body and the mind, both slaves of desires. We totally forget the spiritual flight that we have to take in a desire to fulfill our wishes. But when we fall on this path of life, unable to gather success that we tend to lose patience and become restless. Within the limited parameters of this body when we are face to face with failure, at this juncture, when our dreams are not coming true, we call the Lord from the core of our heart—yes, unfortunately, we selfish souls remember the Lord more or only in times of sorrow or in the difficult phases of life. Its the power of HIS DIVINE NAME that pleases us at this point. The Lord comes running to fulfil our selfish desires, which have fully or totally blinded us. Even when we call Him to satisfy our selfish motives the Lord is Happy as He feels that we mortals, His mere reflection, at last remembered Him, though to fulfil our own desires. This remembrance may be to fulfil our Materialistic needs, to fructify our endless desires—yet the Lord "always" comes whenever we call Him. He puts the ointment of His Name on the seat of pain, fulfilling our material desires to some extent. He shows us the path that leads us to the true mission of our life—unification with the Lord.

We have often heard that the seed of happiness is hidden in sorrow, it is darkness alone that assures, that light will follow, we learn to get up and walk straight only after a fall, similarly its by the Lords Grace alone that we mortals can see or visualize the real mission of our life, i.e., deliverance by riding the vehicle of HIS Name even amid our wants and desires, while yearning for materialism, yet always calling or remembering the Lord. That is why Baba has said, "come take all the help you desire, as what you have asked for is not too far."

We may be asking for fulfilment of our material desires but even behind this is hidden the Lords Divine task, i.e., to turn us towards our true destination, unification with God, and for the same we have to keep chanting His name, always remembering Him.

For example if a child repeatedly makes faults or is adamant over something, still the mother repeatedly makes an attempt to put her child on the right path, even if she has to fulfil one or two wishes of her child but she knows that between love and scolding she will definitely be able to make her child a "good human being". One day her child will give up wrong adamant convictions to make the right choices in life. Same way the Lord also brings us towards the right path paved by Him, by fulfilling our material desires, as the power of HIS Name is such that it makes impossible things possible. The Lord knows very well that we mortals will one day give up the wrong materialistic desires and will be able to move towards our true mission, i.e., unification with the Lord. Even though we humans are ever rapt in this mortal coil, asking for and attaining materialism but our basic that is residing inside us, the Lord Himself pulls us inwards. One day we have to shed off the artificial covering this body to merge into our basic nature, i.e., to attain the Lord Almighty.

So go to the Lords abode, call Him through prayers, keep chanting His Name to attain your material ends but this is a known and experienced reality that Lords Grace is being showered on us even in the attainment of material desires and its by His Grace alone that we are automatically getting a feel of spirituality. Once the joy of His name, the touch or feel of spirituality, the amazing feel of His Grace touches us then we will be able to see and ask for what really should be asked for, i.e., the Lord Himself. This mission, this destination will be visible, with His Grace, it will please the mind and our feet will start becoming stable on the path of spirituality even amid materialism. Most of us go to Shirdi for the fulfilment of our innumerable desires yet His Grace and love is so powerful that we tend to lose our own selves in His Divine love. We sit there in a desire to attain materialism but are so easily and profoundly filled with His love that we don't even come to know and seem to be fully unaware of this divine flow. He surely gives us some chocolates in times of hunger, only to lead us to a stage where life itself becomes a chocolate, i.e., sweetened with HIS DIVINE LOVE.

We called the Lord to fulfil the desires of our mind, desires arising as bondages of the body, He came to us instantaneously, He fulfilled our desires but all the same the touch of the touch stone, the appearance of His name unveiled its true effect. We mortal beings, asking for materialism, are also taking the Lord's name, and its here itself that the seed of spirituality is sown. The touch of this Paras will surely show its effect. The Lords name in our life will surely urge us or fill us with a desire to gather the Lords love, hence pushing us closer to Him. Baba is waiting for us with His arms wide open, He is ever eager to give us His help and support at every step in life as He knows that as we mortals turn towards Him, get His support, then this is surely the first step of spiritual progress in our life. Its God alone who knows and creates this reality for us that while spinning in the cycle of asking and getting from the Lord, we are released from the same to reach the core, our basic—THE LORD. We all are a part of the long queues of temples where we are desirous of HIS prasad in the form of fulfilment of desires in one way or another, yet we unknowingly, by chanting HIS name and with HIS Grace attain HIM, which is purely designed, inspired and fully controlled by the Lord. We, as humans, are used to asking for more and ever more, that is why Baba has said in the Sai Sat Charita that there will be no dearth of food and clothing in His devotees homes, for Him this entire creation is His devotee, so if you need to ask for something, desire and ask only for ME, i.e., the Lord Himself. This is not so easy, amid the five senses and Maya, yet "His Name'" saves us, as the Agasti in the mire of our wants, to lead us to new horizons where we "WANT ONLY HIM".

So, "Come and take full Help from Me"—the help may be in the form of material goods, of Maya but all the same the Lord's name will touch our lips, we will remember Him and once HIS Name and HIS remembrance pleases our inner self then it will surely show its effect and confirm, "that whatever you have asked for is not too far."

This fact may keep filling us with materialism but will also lead us to the threshold of spirituality, enhancing us towards what we should really ask for in life, i.e., the Lord Himself. Maybe, at this juncture we, who are like inverted

pots, not ready to take what the Lord wants to give, may turn the right way, i.e., with the mouth open or turned upwards, to receive what the Lord really wants to fill in us—we will attain our true mission—the Lord. We will take the spiritual flight, filled with the Lords love, to ultimately merge into love itself and love is nothing but God or as we say "GOD is love".
So be it!
Om Sai Ram!

Tenth Promise

I will never be able to pay his debt,
who is always rapt in Me.

Lord, God, Allah, Ishwar are different names of the power above us, who has created this entire creation, He alone looks after the well being of His creation, i.e., reins the show of the Universe and ultimately He alone takes away life from His own creation, to once again recreate. He alone takes different forms and comes down to earth, by making Maya, Nature a means for the same. He makes His beings tread the path of Karma and devotion and its through these innumerable forms that he creates innumerable Leelas for our upliftment. He Himself appears in an incarnated form and introduces innumerable beings on this earth to His true self through this incarnated form, so that we mortals, born of Maya and who are always surrounded by Maya, get a knock to wake up, by His Divine touch and hence, a desire to search our own true identity is ignited. We mortals are always swayed by our own Karmic entanglements, in a never ending race of materialism. We do remember the Lord, chant His Name but only for our own bodily, material, worldly pleasures, for our own comfort, peace and harmony. But the sun rises with an assurance to disintegrate darkness, it has to, as no darkness can sustain itself on the arrival of light. Similarly on the accumulation of some good deeds in our life, the divine Sun of the Lord's Name, His Grace enters our life and this is a sure sign for the darkness of Maya to slowly vanish. Hence we mortals start moving on this path of life filled with the Lords love, His devotion, with His support and by being fully rapt in His thoughts and divine feel. Slowly with the passage of time, even amid materialism, due to the effect of the Lord's Name, His divine light starts radiating from within, i.e., this body made of five elements starts radiating the true self hidden inside us onto our outer form too. The Sun of the Lords Grace enters our life on the threshold of love and devotion. We mortals seem to be moving towards the true mission of our life, i.e., Unification of the soul with the super soul and undoubtedly this path is lighted for us by the Lords Name, shower of His love and His Grace alone. The Lords Light is filled with Divine peace and harmony, that once we get a feel of the same, we are eager to gather more and more in the casket of our life. So we mortals, who always want material things, once again call the Lord, yearning for His divine glimpse, to get a feel of His touch, to bathe in the Bliss of His Divine Joy. The focus slowly turns from materialistic gains to attain the joy of the Lord, as we mortals keep yearning for happiness, contentment, peace of one kind or another, all our lives.

We mortals, while asking for and attaining material things do get the same by His Grace but all the same we get a feel of the Lord's joy, the magical peace giving touch, feel of the Lord. The feel that we get on the Lord's arrival, which we bodily beings can understand—as Lord is actually always with us, is full of a different kind of happiness, eternal peace, and unknowingly it fills our inner self with Divine Bliss. We mortals are bound by maya, hence we feel that this happiness, this contentment is of material gains but actually, without our being able to realize this fact, this joy is of the Lord's arrival in the cover of Maya. The Lord who appeared to satisfy our material desires but because of His own true nature, He filled our inner self with Divine joy and contentment. We mistake this satiation to be materialistic, hence we are eager to ask for more material things and all our lives spin in this never ending eddy to fulfil our material desires. With the fulfilment of every desire our inner self feels contented which is actually the satiation of the Lord's touch in the guise to fulfil our material wants. Slowly while fulfilling our mayavi desires we unknowingly start enjoying the Godly joy flowing to us through His Name and its then that the filth of maya disintegrates, the night of darkness is lost, hence giving birth to our true self, i.e., the Godly feel seeps in. Then unknowingly even while asking for material goods, we are filled with devotional love, in fact we actually start falling in love with the Divine love, i.e., God. We want to get a feel of His enlightening appearance. When the tables turn, it is amazing, i.e., the ones who were always desirous of Maya now want to get a feel of Mayapati alone. The joy that we get on the Lords divine touch, His appearance in our lives, is much more satiating than material gains, in fact there is no comparison. So now we start growing in the Lords love, progress on the threshold of this love and are ever eager to get a glimpse of His loving countenance, hence we call and yearn for HIM, filled with love and devotion. The Lord responds to our call of love and devotion, He grants us the satiation of His Divine Glimpse, putting to rest our yearning for His touch, His love. The tears that a devotee sheds for His Lord, in a heart felt desire to be one with HIM are not waste, as they are adorned by the Lord Himself, as though He comes and resides inside us through our eyes, bound by the thread of our tears that have been shed for HIS love. So when a materialistic being is transformed into the fortunate devotee, each pore of our body is filled with the Lord's love, we don't even come to know, and this is fully and completely the effect of the Lord's Grace alone. A devotee whose entire self is radiating only the Lord's name, such a devotee is only a reflection of His Lord, hence is fully illuminated by and radiating His Lords light.

A devotee who is ever chanting His Name, is rapt in the Lords love, is ever eager to get the Lord's glimpse, the Lord too is in search of such a devotee. The Lord is indebted to such a devotee as He cannot stay away from such loving devotion shown towards Him, He is always seen around His devotee, tied to His love. That is why Sai Baba has said, "I will never be able to pay his debt, who is always rapt in me."

A devotee whose speech is always filled with the Lord's name, if he speaks at all, its His Lord's name and sings His praise, the one who not only fills his inner self with joy by treading the path shown by the Lord but also tries to fill, the Lord's true love in the hearts of one and all by spreading Lords messages, through the medium of "The Lord's Name" alone. The words of a fortunate or blessed devotee always thank the Lord in times of joy, in the balanced phases of life he always sings the praise of the Lord and calls the Lord alone in his times of sorrow or dumps. He crosses the stage of cribbing and cravings, in all situations of life. He is pleased and in tune with the Lords name, His love and devotion in His Lotus feet, in the race of Karmas, in every deed he performs, its the Lord's name alone that is his respite or that pleases him, taking or holding onto the Lord's name as the string of his life, he is stuck to the same. The mind of such a one is always linked with the Lord. While performing one's deeds, while performing all bodily functions such a one is always linked to the Lord internally, i.e., the mind is rapt in the Lord alone. The body may fall or rise, whatever be the bodily deed, at that juncture but the mind is always engrossed in the Lords name, His pious feel. If we perform all our deeds rapt in His name then it would be difficult to discriminate between the Lord and His devotee because if the Lord is ever alive in the casket of our heart, He alone is shining from within ceaselessly then He alone is our true identity, He alone is radiating all around us, He alone is appealing and satisfying our mind by radiating His true self from our inner self.

When the Lord is the basis of our words, is fully seated in our mind, then the body is a mere puppet to the command of our mind and it will automatically move towards the Lord, as directed by our mind. Such a person will always be rapt in the Lord, wherever he or she may be—in a temple or a party or anywhere else, even amid a crowd such a one will be engrossed in his or her inner self, even amid bodily Karmas its the Lord's presence in and around us that will elate us when we will move towards the Lord with our mind, words, body and Karmas—all is directed towards the Lord. We are only desirous to attain the Lord, love Him alone and aim to live on the want of being one with Him. When our mind, our thoughts, words and bodily deeds are all rapt in the Lord's name then the Lord will surely come and be stationed in our body, with His divinity, His divine indivisible self will glitter, hence illuminating the feel of "I am Shiva" in us, i.e., the difference between the devotee and the Lord will go on reducing and the devotee too will adorn the identity of His Guru, to be one with Him or to be seen as His reflection alone. Whenever one would take the Lord's name, such a devotee will also be in our hearts, as a reflection of the Lord alone or in other words the company of such a dedicated devotee will put us on the path of the Lord.

When the devotee is fully rapt in His Lord with His mind, words and bodily self, i.e., one has fully merged his identity into that of his Lord then how can the Lord ever pay the debt of such a being as now both, i.e., the Lord and devotee, are "one" and not two different or separate entities and we only pay the debt of another being, not our own selves. In the peace giving moment of unification of the Lord and the devotee its Sai alone who shines in His devotee and the devotee gets the honor of being one with His Lord Sai.

This body crosses the parameters of the debts of give and take that bind us and our entire self finds an entry into our true selves and its after this point of elation that we are one with the Lord, i.e., a sense of Shivo Ham radiates and hence smiles with satiation and peace for ever and ever and ever......

Embrace SAI, seat Him in the casket of your heart with your mind, body deeds, speech, i.e., completely, that even while dwelling in this body our soul gets a feel of being liberated, crossing the gives and takes, the debts of this body and hence the soul merges into the super soul. When the feel of being "one" with the Lord shines in our lives then the Karmic give and take will slow down or will seem to come to a halt as these feelings of duality only arise when we are not one with the Lord and live as separate or different entities on the threshold of being "one" with the Lord. A devotee then seems to be fully a reflection of Sai or in other words the devotee fully merges into the Lord, then how can we have the parameter of debts, of give and take with our own selves?

Know and realize this fact, understand each vicissitude, in and out of your life. Fill your entire self with the Lord's name and in this feel of unification with the Lord, at the pious juncture where we embrace deliverance, just smile with a countenance that reflects the face of your Guru God Sai and sure enough you will be identified as and called the reflection of "Sai" and "Sai" alone.

So be it!
Om Sai Ram!

Eleventh Promise

*That devotee is great who
has no other refuge but 'ME'.*

It is commonly said that to realize one's mistake is a step to progress in life. A devotee who is fully merged in his Karmic cycle gets a respite by taking the Lord's name, hence putting in order the jigsaw puzzle of life and its with the Lord's Grace alone that we mortals, who are spinning in a cycle of 84 lakh forms, realize our true self, to finally merge into the Lord. Similarly a devotee is great whose life is not only a gift of the Lord but His entire life is based on the Lord's Grace alone. Such a one accepts or adorns each phase or gift in life as His grace alone and making the boat of His Name, such a devotee finds the final deliverance of life in the Lord's Lotus feet alone, merging into his true identity, i.e., the Lord.

We have been granted this mortal coil by the coming together of the five elements of nature namely, air, water, earth, sky and fire and its the Lord's identity as the soul which gives this dead coil—"life". The Lord played a wonderful game—He detached Himself from His own self, hence binding Himself to the parameters of a body, dancing in 84 lakh forms—one after the other and created this cycle for His own self, i.e., the soul to reach His own Divine self, i.e., the super soul. We mortals are bound to the parameters of the body and hence are fully deluded by Maya. We mortals take only that as the reality of life—the things we can see or touch, hence, we mortals, born of Maya are fully engulfed by Maya, deluded by Maya. We have lost the light within to the darkness of Maya, as we are unable to recognize the unseen, untouched life in us, our soul and keep wandering, in the glitter of names and forms alone.

In the race for Maya, in a madness to attain only materialistic ends, when the strings of our mind dance at the knock on the door of our inner self, a knock by the Lord Himself, that we get a feel of the light inside. When we mortals are surrounded by sorrow that we get a feel of the power within,, i.e., the Lord, as we remember and call Him with an earnest self to free us of our sorrow. As we have been created from the earth and are bound to this body that will perish one day, hence only the perishable pleases us and its the material goods that we yearn for all our life, in fact life after life. We go to the temple, regularly, bow our head for 40 days regularly in front of the Lord, read religious scriptures, perform big rituals but all are based on a desire to "gain" something from the Lord. Even in the spiritual flight we try to gather materialism alone—wanting and asking for the same. In this race for Maya, materialism, satisfying our own me and mine, when the effects of Maya surface, when this body or mind suffers the effects of its own negative Karmas, then in this painful situation created by Maya, we call the Lord, pray to Him to free us from this pain. The call is due to the painful, suffering of the vagrant mind. At this juncture we get a feel of the reality that Maya ultimately leads us to pain and the reward of the Lords Name alone is joy, eternal joy. Probably that is why we get a feel, a glimpse of the true nature of the Lord, i.e., the beginning of joy and end of sorrow. We get a feel of the joy and experience the same when the Lord appears (not bodily)—as an annihilator from sorrow. After entering the Divine threshold of the Lord's abode, in His Divine feel we dance in joy to merge in the indivisible joy. After bathing in this joy some beings are eager to attain and move closer to the Lord by increasing the chanting of the Lords name but most of us would probably just bathe in this joy, finding freedom from the sorrow and once again become rapt or lost in Maya. We fools do get a feel of the Divine Grace but once again regress to sit back amid Maya. This totally depends on our Karmic cycle and when will the Lord's Grace fall on which soul, is fully and entirely ordained by the Lord.

After attaining the Lord's Grace, to lose oneself in that Grace is the fortune of a few pious souls, as it adorns only a few, the rest choose darkness even after attaining joy, even after getting the feel of the Lord they keep wandering in the comforts of the mortal coil alone, hence accepting darkness, digression as their fate.

Those fortunate souls that wake up on the Lord's tap, are filled with joy of spirituality on the Lord's touch, hence aiming towards their deliverance in chanting the Lord's name alone, such souls are really "great", as even amid Maya they are not engulfed fully by Maya though it surely troubles them due to the bodily feel. Such beings bathe in atmic elation even while dwelling in this body. Even though bound by Maya, they attain the Lord by the power of His name and His Grace alone. So those beings who, while living in this world, performing all worldly deeds, experience joy and sorrow due to the effect of Maya, yet its the Lord's Name alone that pleases them, its solely their faith in the Lord and His divine support that makes them move ahead in life, such souls only need the oar of the Lord's name, while engulfed by the flood of Maya. Such a one definitely gets the Lord's Grace and is considered Great even by the Lord. For example we need food when we are hungry, water alone can quench our thirst, joy alone puts an end to sorrow, one desirous of Maya can only dance to the jingling sound of coins. But a rare one wants, yearns and calls for the Lord alone in all situations—hunger, thirst, joy or sorrow. Such a one alone wants to "always" get a "feel" of His Lord, such a devotee is very dear to the Lord, is great.

So in every situation of life, in all conditions created by Maya, in every juncture of life, when surrounded by sorrow or in every spiritual flight we take amid the mire of Maya, the one who always, at all times, every minute, with every breath chants only the Lord's name, calls only the Lord and loves the Lord earnestly, sheds tears only in His devotion, such a devotee becomes "great". Such a one is special as he or she has been born of Maya, grown in Maya, will ultimately lose oneself in Maya and will be reborn in Maya, once again will keep spinning in a wheel of 84 lakh types of creations, amid these polluted attractions, surrounded by the intoxication of Maya, yet only the Lords Grace, being close to His abode gives peace to such a one. Its the Lords name alone that gets a glow on such a devotees face, the one who loses himself or herself in Lords devotion, His love and nothing else pleases such a one, he finds joy only in losing himself in the Lords lap as he knows nothing else but the Lord, such a one indeed is a "great" devotee.

When life is filled with joy we thank the Lord, when difficulties surround us, we call only the Lord, when we cook food that we offer it to Him, filled with His name alone, when we dance in joy it seems as though the Lords abode is smiling on us, when our mind is vagrant that we offer our mind at His Lotus feet and are adorned by the ornament of peace. Come what may, in all actions in life—big or small, we only worship call, thank, yearn, remember, God. It seems as though He is tied to each breath we take. When its only His Name that is an integral part of every incoming and outgoing breath, each pore of our body is filled with His Name alone, even while dwelling in this body created by maya, that yearns only for Maya, yet its the Lord's Name alone that pleases us, elates our inner self, then such a rare soul which is pleased and bathes in the joy of His protective embrace alone, such a devotee surely bathes in the proud moment of being one with His Guru, His God. Such a one who has attained the "Divine Glow" of the Lord even while dwelling in this body, is rare, is "Great" as such a one has attained the rare, amazing, unparalleled, joyous Grace of the Lord. Our mortal coil is "Great" only if it is able to understand the true form of the Lord, adorned His true self and merged into its true self. This is only possible if we mortals have worshipped God with each incoming and outgoing breath, have worshipped "Him" alone, have Loved the Lord and at all times have sought the refuge of His protective embrace, His Grace. That "Life" indeed is "Great" that has smiled always as a reflection of God, the one life that has attained its true self in the Lords Grace alone, losing himself or herself in this Divinity, the one to whom this world has never appealed yet is fully influenced, yearns and is in tune not with the world but is rapt in the creator of the same. Such a devotee is really Great and rare who has no place of rest or refuge in this world except Sai, Sai and Sai alone.

So be it!

Om Sai Ram

● ● ●

Our Books on SHIRDI SAI BABA

Shirdi Sai Baba is a household name in India as well as in many parts of the World today. These books offer fascinating glimpses into the life and miracles of Shirdi Sai Baba and other Perfect Masters. These books will provide you with an experience that is bound to transform one's sense of perspective and bring about perceptible and meaningful spiritual growth.

Shirdi Sai Baba: The Universal Master
Sri Kaleshwar
978 81 207 9664 5
₹150

A Divine Journey with Baba
Vinny Chitluri
ISBN 978 81 207 9859 5
₹200

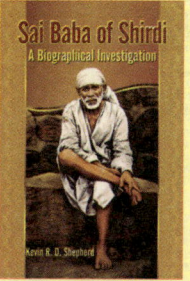

Sai Baba of Shirdi: A Biographical Investigation
Kevin R. D. Shepherd
978 81 207 9899 1
₹450

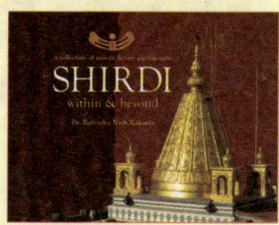

SHIRDI within & beyond
A collection of unseen & rare photographs
Dr. Rabinder Nath Kakarya
ISBN 978 81 207 7806 1
₹750

The Eternal Sai Consciousness
A. R. Nanda
ISBN 978 81 207 9043 8
₹200

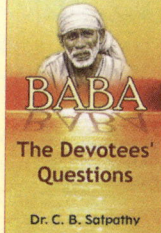

BABA: The Devotees' Questions
Dr. C. B. Satpathy
ISBN 978 81 207 8966 1
₹150

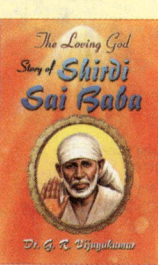

The Loving God: Story of Shirdi Sai Baba
Dr. G. R. Vijayakumar
ISBN 978 81 207 8079 8
₹200

Sai Samartha and Ramana Maharshi
S. Seshadri
ISBN 978 81 207 8986 9
₹150

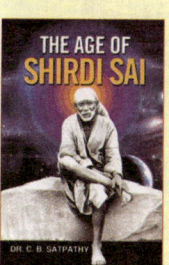

The Age of Shirdi Sai
Dr. C. B. Satpathy
ISBN 978 81 207 8700 1
₹225

Message of Shri Sai
Suresh Chandra Panda
ISBN 978 81 207 9512 9
₹150

Sree Sai Charitra Darshan
Mohan Jagannath Yadav
ISBN 978 81 207 8346 1
₹200

Shri Sai Baba Teachings & Philosophy
Lt Col M B Nimbalkar
ISBN 978 81 207 2364 1
₹100

STERLING

SHIRDI SAI BABA

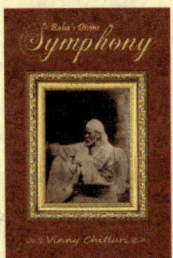
Baba's Divine Symphony
Vinny Chitluri
ISBN 978 81 207 8485 7
₹ 250

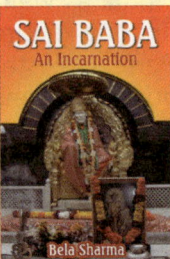
Sai Baba an Incarnation
Bela Sharma
ISBN 978 81 207 8833 6
₹ 200

**Shirdi Sai Baba:
The Perfect Master**
*Suresh Chandra Panda &
Smita Panda*
ISBN 978 81 207 8113 9
₹ 200

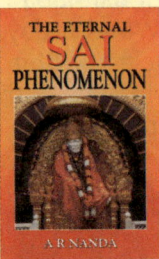
**The Eternal Sai
Phenomenon**
A R Nanda
ISBN 978 81 207 6086 8
₹ 200

**Baba's Rinanubandh
Leelas during His Sojourn in Shirdi**
Compiled by Vinny Chitluri
ISBN 978 81 207 3403 6
₹ 200

**Baba's Gurukul
SHIRDI**
Vinny Chitluri
ISBN 978 81 207 4770 8
₹ 200

**Baba's Anurag
Love for His Devotees**
Compiled by Vinny Chitluri
ISBN 978 81 207 5447 8
₹ 125

**Baba's Vaani: His Sayings and
Teachings**
Compiled by Vinny Chitluri
ISBN 978 81 207 3859 1
₹ 200

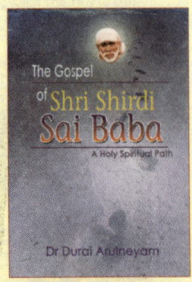
**The Gospel of Shri Shirdi Sai
Baba: A Holy Spiritual Path**
Dr Durai Arulneyam
ISBN 978 81 207 3997 0
₹ 150

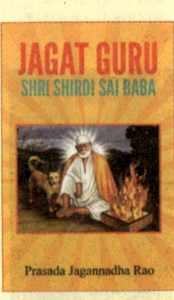
**Jagat Guru: Shri Shirdi
Sai Baba**
Prasada Jagannadha Rao
ISBN 978 81 207 8175 7
₹ 100

Spotlight on the Sai Story
Chakor Ajgaonker
ISBN 978 81 207 4399 1
₹ 125

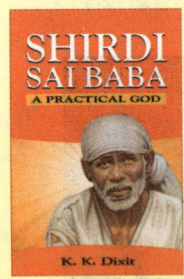
**Shirdi Sai Baba
A Practical God**
K. K. Dixit
ISBN 978 81 207 5918 3
₹ 75

STERLING

Sab Ka Malik Ek

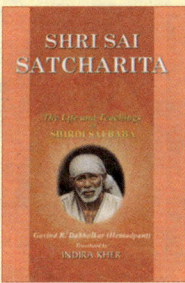

Shri Sai Satcharita
The Life and Teachings of Shirdi Sai Baba
Translated by Indira Kher
ISBN 978 81 207 2211 8 ₹ 550(HB)
ISBN 978 81 207 2153 1 ₹ 450(PB)

Shirdi Sai Baba
The Divine Healer
Raj Chopra
ISBN 978 81 207 4766 1
₹ 100

Shirdi Sai Baba and other Perfect Masters
C B Satpathy
ISBN 978 81 207 2384 9
₹ 150

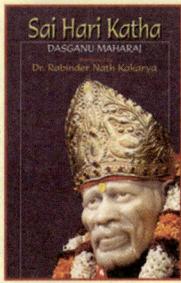

Sai Hari Katha
Dasganu Maharaj Translated by
Dr. Rabinder Nath Kakarya
ISBN 978 81 207 3324 4
₹ 100

Unravelling the Enigma: Shirdi Sai Baba in the light of Sufism
Marianne Warren
ISBN 978 81 207 2147 0
₹ 400

I am always with you
Lorraine Walshe-Ryan
ISBN 978 81 207 3192 9
₹ 150

BABA- May I Answer
C.B. Satpathy
ISBN 978 81 207 4594 0
₹ 150

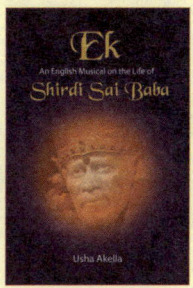

Ek An English Musical on the Life of Shirdi Sai Baba
Usha Akella
ISBN 978 81 207 6842 0
₹ 75

Sri Sai Baba
Sai Sharan Anand
Translated by V.B Kher
ISBN 978 81 207 1950 7
₹ 200

Sai Baba: His Divine Glimpses
V B Kher
ISBN 978 81 207 2291 0
₹ 95

A Diamond Necklace To: Shirdi Sai Baba
Giridhar Ari
ISBN 978 81 207 5868 1
₹ 200

Life History of Shirdi Sai Baba
Ammula Sambasiva Rao
ISBN 978 81 207 7722 4
₹ 200

STERLING

SHIRDI SAI BABA

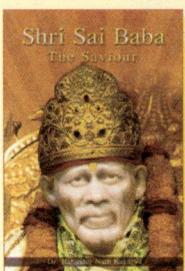

Shri Sai Baba- The Saviour
Dr. Rabinder Nath Kakarya
ISBN 978 81 207 4701 2
₹ 100

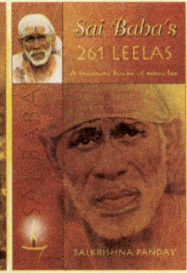

Sai Baba's 261 Leelas
Balkrishna Panday
ISBN 978 81 207 2727 4
₹ 125

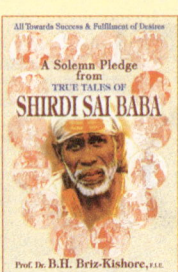

A Solemn Pledge from True Tales of Shirdi Sai Baba
Dr B H Briz-Kishore
ISBN 978 81 207 2240 8
₹ 95

God Who Walked on Earth: The Life & Times of Shirdi Sai Baba
Rangaswami Parthasarathy
ISBN 978 81 207 1809 8
₹ 150

Shri Shirdi Sai Baba: His Life and Miracles
ISBN 978 81 207 2877 6
₹ 30

The Miracles of Sai Baba
ISBN 978 81 207 5433 1 (HB)
₹ 250

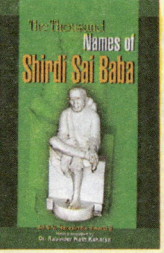

The Thousand Names of Shirdi Sai Baba
Sri B.V. Narasimha Swami Ji
Hindi translation by
Dr. Rabinder Nath Kakarya
ISBN 978 81 207 3738 9
₹ 75

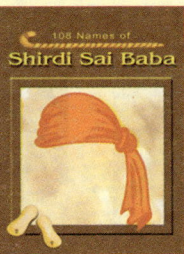

108 Names of Shirdi Sai Baba
ISBN 978 81 207 3074 8
₹ 50

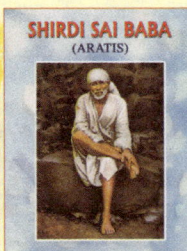

Shirdi Sai Baba Aratis
ISBN 978 81 207 8456 7
(English)   ₹ 10

Shirdi Sai Speaks... Sab Ka Malik Ek
Quotes for the Day
ISBN 978 81 207 3101 1
₹ 200

Divine Gurus

Guru Charitra
Shree Swami Samarth
ISBN 978 81 207 3348 0
₹ 200

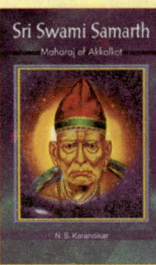

Sri Swami Samarth Maharaj of Akkalkot
N.S. Karandikar
ISBN 978 81 207 3445 6
₹ 200

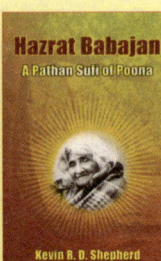

Hazrat Babajan: A Pathan Sufi of Poona
Kevin R. D. Shepherd
ISBN 978 81 207 8698 1
₹ 200

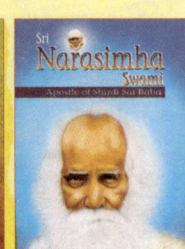

Sri Narasimha Swami Apostle of Shirdi Sai Baba
Dr. G.R. Vijayakumar
ISBN 978 81 207 4432 5
₹ 90

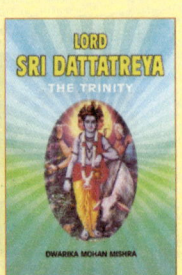

Lord Sri Dattatreya The Trinity
Dwarika Mohan Mishra
ISBN 978 81 207 5417 1
₹ 200

STERLING

श्री शिरडी साई बाबा

जेल में साई साक्षात्कार
राकेश जुनेजा
978 81 207 9507 5
₹ 150

श्री साई चरित्र दर्शन
मोहन जगन्नाथ यादव
978 81 207 8350 8
₹ 200

श्री साई सच्चरित्र
श्री शिरडी साई बाबा की अद्भुत जीवनी तथा उनके अमूल्य उपदेश
गोविंद रघुनाथ दाभोलकर (हेमाडपंत)
978 81 207 2500 3   ₹ 300 (HB)

शिरडी अंत: से अनंत
डॉ. रबिन्द्रनाथ ककरिया
978 81 207 8191 7
₹ 750

साई सुमिरन
अंजु टंडन
978 81 207 8706 3
₹ 90

बाबा की वाणी-उनके वचन तथा आदेश
बेला शर्मा
978 81 207 4745 6
₹ 100

बाबा का अनुराग
विनी चितलुरी
978 81 207 6699 0
₹ 100

बाबा का ऋणानुबंध
विनी चितलुरी
978 81 207 5998 5
₹ 150

बाबा का गुरुकुल-शिरडी
विनी चितलुरी
978 81 207 6698 3
₹ 125

साई की आत्मकथा
विकास कपूर
978 81 207 7719 4
₹ 200

बाबा-आध्यात्मिक विचार
चन्द्रभानु सतपथी
978 81 207 4627 5
₹ 150

पृथ्वी पर अवतरित भगवान शिरडी के साई बाबा
रंगस्वामी पार्थसारथी
978 81 207 2101 2
₹ 150

श्री शिरडी साईं बाबा

श्री शिरडी साईं बाबा एवं अन्य सद्गुरु
चन्द्रभानु सतपथी
978 81 207 4401 1
₹ 90

साईं शरण में
चन्द्रभानु सतपथी
978 81 207 2802 8
₹ 150

साईं – सबका मालिक
कल्पना भाकुनी
978 81 207 9886 1
₹ 200

साईं बाबा एक अवतार
बेला शर्मा
978 81 207 6706 5
₹ 100

साईं सत् चरित का प्रकाश
बेला शर्मा
978 81 207 7804 7
₹ 200

श्री साईं बाबा के परम भक्त
डॉ. रबिन्द्रनाथ ककरिया
978 81 207 2779 3
₹ 75

श्री साईं बाबा के उपदेश व तत्त्वज्ञान
लेफ्टिनेन्ट कर्नल एम. बी. निंबालकर
978 81 207 5971 8   ₹ 100

साईं भक्तानुभव
डॉ. रबिन्द्रनाथ ककरिया
978 81 207 3052 6
₹ 125

श्री साईं बाबा के अनन्य भक्त
डॉ. रबिन्द्र नाथ ककरिया
978 81 207 2705 2
₹ 100

साईं का संदेश
डॉ. रबिन्द्र नाथ ककरिया
978 81 207 2879 0
₹ 125

शिरडी संपूर्ण दर्शन
डॉ. रबिन्द्रनाथ ककरिया
978 81 207 2312 2
₹ 50

मुक्तिदाता – श्री साईं बाबा
डॉ. रबिन्द्रनाथ ककरिया
978 81 207 2778 6
₹ 65

सबका मालिक एक

साई दत्तावधूता
राजेन्द्र भण्डारी
978 81 207 4400 4
₹ 75

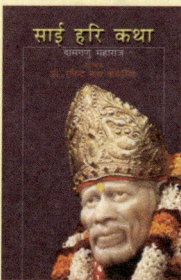

साई हरि कथा
दासगणु महाराज
978 81 207 3323 7
₹ 65

श्री नरसिम्हा स्वामी
शिरडी साई बाबा के
दिव्य प्रचारक
डॉ. रबिन्द्र नाथ ककरिया
978 81 207 4437 0   ₹ 75

**शिरडी साई बाबा - की सत्य
कथाओं से प्राप्त - एक पावन
प्रतिज्ञा**
प्रो. डॉ. बी.एच. ब्रिज-किशोर
978 81 207 2346 7   ₹ 80

**शिरडी साई बाबा की दिव्य
लीलाएँ**
डॉ. रबिन्द्र नाथ ककरिया
978 81 207 6376 0   ₹ 150

श्री साई चालीसा
978 81 207 4773 9
₹ 50

शिरडी साई बाबा आरती
978 81 207 8195 5
₹ 10

आरती संग्रह (Boardbook)
ISBN 978 81 207 9057 5
Size: 10.70 cm x 15.45 cm
₹ 100

शिरडी साई के दिव्य वचन-सब का मालिक एक
प्रतिदिन का विचार
978 81 207 3533 0
₹ 180

स्टर्लिंग

श्री शिरडी साई बाबा

Oriya Language

ଶ୍ରୀ ସାଇ ସଚରିତ୍ର (Oriya)
ଶ୍ରୀ ଗୋବିନ୍ଦରାଓ ରଘୁନାଥ ଦାଭୋଳକର
(ହେମାଡପନ୍ତ)
978 81 207 8332 4   ₹ 300

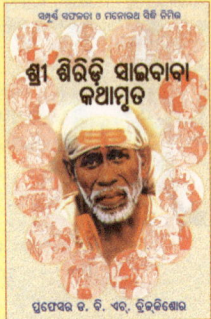
ଶ୍ରୀ ଶିରିଡ଼ି ସାଇବାବା କଥାମୃତ
ପ୍ରଫେସର ଜ. ବି. ଏନ. ବୃଜକିଶୋର (Oriya)
978 81 207 7774 3
₹ 80

ଶିରୁଡ଼ି ସାଇ ବାବାଙ୍କ ଜୀବନ ଚରିତ (Oriya)
ଅନୁବାଦକ ଶାରଦୀନ ରାଓ
ଅନୁବାଦକ - କିଶୋର ଚନ୍ଦ୍ର ପଟ୍ଟନାୟକ
978 81 207 7417 9   ₹125

Other Indian Languages

షిరిడీసాయిబాబా (Telugu)
प्रो. डॉ. बी.एच. ब्रिज-किशोर
978 81 207 2294 1
₹ 80

ಶ್ರೀ ಶಿರಡಿ ಸಾಯಿಬಾಬಾ ಅವರ (Kannada)
प्रो. डॉ. बी.एच. ब्रिज-किशोर
978 81 207 2873 8
₹ 80

ஷிரடி சாயிபாபாவின் (Tamil)
உண்மைக்கதைகளிலிருந்து பெறுமதியான வாக்குறுதி
प्रो. डॉ. बी.एच. ब्रिज-किशोर
978 81 207 2876 9
₹80

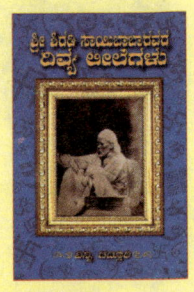
978 81 207 8930 2
₹225

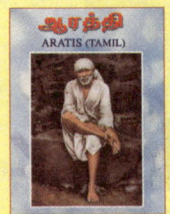
Shirdi Sai Baba Aratis
(Tamil)   ₹ 10

Shirdi Sai Baba Aratis
(Telugu)   ₹ 10

Shirdi Sai Baba Aratis
(Kannada)   ₹ 10

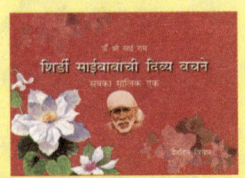
शिर्डी साईबाबांची दिव्य वचने (Marathi)
सबका मालिक एक
दैनंदिन विचार
978 81 207 7518 3   ₹ 180

STERLING PUBLISHERS PVT. LTD.
Regd. Office: A-59, Okhla Industrial Area, Phase-II, New Delhi-110020, CIN: U22110PB1964PTC002569
For Online order & detailed Catalogue visit our website:
www.sterlingpublishers.com, E-mail : mail@sterlingpublishers.com, Tel. 91-11-26386165, 26387070